TORTURED WITH LOVE

TORTURED WITH LOVE

The True Crime Romance of the Lonely Hearts Killers

J.T. HUNTER

Pedialaw Press

Copyright

ISBN-13: 9780578720289

Cover design by: Art Painter
Formatting and Layout by: Evening Sky Publishing Services

Library of Congress Control Number: 2018675309

Printed in the United States of America

Dedication

This book is dedicated to JBW with my own tortured love.

Contents

Part Three

"My story is a love story, but only those tortured with love can understand what I mean."

- Martha Beck, Sing Sing Prison

Preface

The "strange, lurid case" of Martha Beck and Raymond Fernandez, dubbed the "Lonely Hearts Killers" by the media, so captured the consciousness of the American public that they rank fourth on *Time* magazine's list of the Top 10 Crime Duos in U.S. History. (Only Bonnie & Clyde, Butch Cassidy & the Sundance Kid, and Frank & Jesse James come before them).

In his discussion of the Lonely Hearts Killers, author Bruce Sanders described them as the "most incredible lovers in the twentieth century, people belonging to a nightmare, living characters no novelist or playwright could employ in a plot with any presence of reality, and yet they were real enough, horribly so."

The story of Martha Beck and Raymond Fernandez is a true crime romance, however horrible or incredible it may be.

Part One

I'm nobody's baby, I wonder why
Each night and day I pray the Lord up above
Please send me down somebody to love
But nobody wants me, I'm blue somehow
Won't someone hear my plea
And take a little chance with me
Because I'm nobody's baby now.

"I'm Nobody's Baby" - Marion Harris 1921

Chapter One

On an otherwise mundane March day, a peculiar piece of paper arrived in Martha Beck's office mailbox. It came with the usual medical correspondence and junk mail, giving no indication of its importance. Yet, this one particular envelope would change Martha's life forever.

The envelope arrived on a cool afternoon, the temperature hovering just below 60, the highest it had climbed all day in the Pensacola area of the Florida Panhandle. But Martha was not in the mood to enjoy the weather. She was still down in the dumps about her recently finalized divorce from Alfred Beck, a Pensacola bus driver who had married her when she was six months pregnant with another man's child. Although she had been separated from Alfred since May 1945, nearly two years earlier, the formal entry of their divorce had the nearly 27-year-old Martha feeling like an old maid doomed to live out the rest of her life alone. Martha was not unique in that respect in post-World War II America. With well over a million more women than men, the United States population of the mid and late 1940's left many lonely women in its wake.

A visit from Elizabeth Swanson, one of the nurses she supervised at the Crippled Children's Home, temporarily distracted Martha from

4 • TORTURED WITH LOVE

feeling sorry for herself. She considered Elizabeth her closest friend. When Elizabeth knocked on her office door, Martha had just started going through the mail. As the two engaged in the latest gossip and friendly chit-chat, Martha resumed sorting through the assortment of envelopes. The first was an advertisement from a Jacksonville company selling medical equipment. She quickly flipped past it as well as a few other pieces of junk mail until a mysterious envelope caught her eye. It was made of thin, pale-brown paper with the name, *Mrs. Martha Jule Beck*, typed prominently on the front.

"What's this?" she asked, the question directed more to herself than her friend.

"What is what?" Elizabeth replied, sipping from a mug of coffee.

"This...this odd envelope," Martha said, holding it up to show her.

"Beat's me," Elizabeth remarked coyly. "I wonder who sent you that."

"I'm sure I don't know," Martha remarked, her curiosity now piqued. She turned the envelope over to inspect it further, and seeing nothing hinting at its contents, opened it to find a thin, paper pamphlet inside. It was a promotional mailing and application for the Standard Correspondence Club, one of many "lonely hearts clubs" operating across the country. The return address gave Standard's location as Grave Lake, Illinois.

LONELY?, the pamphlet asked in large, bold letters. *Let us help you find that certain someone. Join old reliable Club, 50 years of dependable, confidential service. Correspondents most everywhere seeking congenial mates, proven results. Interesting photos, descriptions FREE.* There were several pictures of women spaced throughout the page, each next to a testimonial about a happy marriage brought about by contacts made through the club.

"Now why on earth would they send this to me?" Martha wondered aloud, taking a little offense that such a "lovelorn club" would be contacting her. Elizabeth's coyness now morphed into a broad grin that spread across her face.

"I have a confession to make," Elizabeth said as she started giggling. "I wrote the club and asked them to send you information and an application."

Martha studied her friend's face, deciding whether she was serious.

"Whatever for?" she asked in a tone matching the astonishment in her eyes.

Still giggling, Elizabeth moved to a chair closer to Martha and sat down beside her.

"I originally did it as a joke," she explained, "but the more I thought about it, the more I decided that you should give it a try. Three of my daughters are writing to me that they have met men through this correspondence club, and this is the very same club that I met my husband through thirty years ago. And after all, what do you have to lose?"

Martha rolled her eyes.

"I may be a little lonely," she acknowledged, "but I'm not THAT desperate." She glared with some annoyance at Elizabeth. "I swear, sometimes I really wonder what's going on in that head of yours."

Martha tossed the pamphlet onto a pile of papers stacked on the side of her desk and made no more mention of it for the rest of their time together. But the seeds of intrigue had already been planted in her mind.

Later, after Elizabeth had left, Martha retrieved the discarded pamphlet and read it more closely. Part of the pamphlet contained a form asking her to fill out information about herself and write a letter detailing what kind of men she would like to meet. Sitting down at her desk, she carefully completed the form and took her time crafting the letter, being sure to mention how people often commented that she was *witty, vivacious, and oozed personality*. She also emphasized that she was a trained nurse with her own *pleasant apartment*. When she was satisfied with what she had written, Martha carefully folded the papers, enclosed $5.00 for the required membership fee, and licked the envelope to seal it. That evening, she dropped it in a mailbox on her way home from work.

Years later, when asked whether she had experienced any misgivings about joining a lonely hearts club, Martha candidly replied, "Yes, as soon as I'd put the letter in the mailbox, I began thinking I'd made a mistake."

Questioned about what kind of man she hoped to meet through the club, Martha took a little more time before answering.

"Well, I don't know," she confessed. "I guess I hadn't thought about it much. But I sure didn't think I'd ever meet anyone like Ray."

Chapter Two

Raymond Martinez Fernandez was born on December 17, 1914 in Honolulu, Hawaii. His father, Joseph Fernandez-Perez, had immigrated to the United States from Spain seeking work as a laborer. When Ray was three, his father moved the family to Bridgeport, Connecticut in pursuit of other employment opportunities. A harsh disciplinarian, the elder Fernandez dominated the family home, often treating Ray as the "black sheep" of the family, and not bothering to hide his disappointment about Ray's undersized physical stature as a boy.

After Ray completed grammar school at the age of fifteen, his father forced him to stay home and work on the family farm instead of continuing on to high school with his friends. That same year Ray had his first run-in with the law, a result of his father's refusal of a simple request. Ray had asked his father if the family could celebrate Thanksgiving like most Americans by having a turkey. The elder Fernandez scoffed at the idea of "wasting money" on a turkey and coldly informed Ray that if he wanted something special for Thanksgiving, then he would have to get it himself. A few nights later, undeterred by his father's response and determined to celebrate the holiday, Ray recruited two friends to help him steal some chickens from a nearby farm. All three thieves were quickly caught and arrested, but Ray's two accomplices were released to their parents' supervision, while Ray's father refused to accept custody of him. Instead, he stood trial at a juvenile facility in Fairfield County Court and pled guilty to stealing chickens worth $28.75 (equivalent to about $450 in 2020 when adjusted for inflation). The court sentenced him to serve 60 days in county jail and imposed a $50 fine along with court costs.

When Ray was seventeen, he moved to Spain with his mother, Frances Morales, relieved to be free from the strict influence of his father who stayed behind in Connecticut. On January 5, 1934, less than two years after relocating to Spain, Ray married Encarnacion Robles, a dark-haired Spanish beauty, in a Catholic ceremony at the cathedral in Orgiva, Spain. Although his father opposed the marriage on grounds the Robles family was poor and offered no dowry, Ray went through with the wedding because the captivating Encarnacion had captured his heart. The newlyweds soon had their first child, giving Ray extra motivation to work long hours and save money so he could afford to move his wife and newborn son to the United States. Everything was going well for the young family until the Spanish Civil War broke out, derailing Ray's plans.

In what would be a prelude to World War I, Republicans loyal to the Second Spanish Republic fought against a revolt by the Nationalists, an alliance of conservatives and Catholics led by a military group under the command of General Francisco Franco. As war spread through the country, Ray contracted typhoid fever and spent nearly five weeks in and out of consciousness.

Once he was healthy enough to leave the hospital, Ray was indentured by Franco's forces and assigned to be a guard in a prison infamous for executing Republican Loyalist prisoners by firing squad. Part of his duties included tying condemned prisoners to each other and loading them onto trucks or vans, which took them to a 200 feet-long, 12 feet-deep ditch located in a remote field. After being ordered into the ditch, the condemned prisoners would be shot. It was not unusual for Ray to send people he knew to their deaths, even friends and neighbors.

When Ray was unable to maintain his composure during one such occasion, an officer in command of the execution squad noticed him crying. Disgusted at the display of weakness, the officer ordered that Ray be tied up with the prisoners and taken with them to a remote field for execution. As the execution squad prepared to fire, Ray stood with the condemned in the ditch where countless others had been killed. He trembled as the squad commander yelled, "Ready...Aim..." But just before the final command, another officer stopped the countdown and pulled Ray out of the ditch. However, Ray's punishment was not over: he was forced to watch the execution of those who remained behind in the pit.

Coerced into fighting with Franco's Nationalist forces, Ray served at the front line of the war for eight months, experiencing traumatic conditions, including the constant stress of facing enemy fire and the horror of seeing – and smelling – hundreds of dead men rotting on the battlefield. Images of "his best friends being killed and bombs exploding all around him" were forever seared in his brain. Frequently facing starvation due to lack of provisions, Ray and other soldiers often resorted to shooting and eating rabbits that nested inside the rotting corpses. After so many days of torment, the war finally ended in early 1939, but the victorious Francoist regime continued to purge anyone associated with the Republic, executing hundreds of thousands of their countrymen in killing fields like the one Ray witnessed while working at the jail.

After the end of the war, Ray found work in the Gibraltar dock-yards run by the British Government. However, peace did not last for long. On September 1, 1939, Germany's invasion of Poland marked the beginning of World War II. Eager to help the Allied cause, Ray contacted British officials to offer his services. He went on to work for the Defense Security Division of British Intelligence as a letter carrier for spies and anti-sabotage agents, and later served as a counter-spy. His supervisors reported that he performed his duties "extremely well," often carrying out dangerous assignments and remaining loyal to the Allies throughout his service.

In December 1945, having endured two wars in less than a decade,

Ray secured passage on the *Empire Jewell*, an oil tanker that was sailing from Spain to Panama and Curacao, before continuing on to its ultimate destination: New York. Ray planned on earning enough money to be eventually pay for the passage of his wife and son so they could join him in America. Yet, Fate once again intervened. The voyage was hardly underway when a strong storm developed during the first day at sea, and the ship began taking on water as giant waves pounded the bow and crashed over the deck. When the ship's water pumps malfunctioned, Ray hurried to the pump room below deck to help repair them. As he stood in the walkway handing tools down to the boatswain and pump man, a massive wave slammed into the ship, sending a deep sheet of water across the deck and knocking a heavy, metal hatch off its hinges with such force that it smashed down onto Ray, striking him on top of his head. The impact from the six-feet high, half-inch thick steel hatch "produced a heavy indentation in the skull high on the forehead" and left a permanent scar over three inches long on Ray's scalp.

Years later, friends and relatives would insist that Ray's personality drastically changed after the accident. He became more aggressive, developed a stronger sexual appetite, and had difficulty at times distinguishing right from wrong.

When the ship reached Curacao, Ray was immediately admitted to the closest hospital. Due to the severity of his injury, he spent four weeks receiving treatment and recovering. Even after being discharged from the hospital, he continued suffering agonizing headaches that would come and go for the rest of his life. He also developed a powerful sex drive and squandered much of his money seeking relief from local prostitutes.

When he was well enough, Ray took a job as a utility man on

another oil tanker, the SS *Santa Clara*, bound for Liverpool, England before continuing on to its final port of call in Mobile, Alabama. In dire need of money, Ray remained on board for a few weeks after docking in Mobile to earn extra pay working as a general ship's steward. When his additional duties were done, Ray began packing up to leave the ship and saw some other members of the crew hiding towels in their baggage. Not thinking twice about it, Ray did the same thing, but he could not stop with just one towel. Unable to resist the impulse, he stuffed multiple sheets, pillows, and towels into his bag. He was caught trying to pass through customs with the stolen government supplies and promptly arrested. Officers at the federal courthouse for the Southern District of Alabama advised him to plead guilty to the theft charges, assuring him that doing so would result in a suspended sentence since the stolen supplies were valued at only $53. Ray followed their advice and entered a guilty plea to the charges. He was not just surprised, but utterly shocked when the judge sentenced him to spend one year in federal prison for attempted theft of the assortment of linens.

While serving his sentence at the Federal Penitentiary in Tallahassee, Florida, Ray developed a friendship with his cellmate, a Haitian man who practiced Voodoo. Spurred on by his new friend, Ray obtained a copy of *The Magic Island*, William Seabrook's classic account of Voodoo in Haiti. Ray quickly became fascinated by its tales of hypnotism and black magic. Eager to put his newly acquired knowledge to work, Ray wrote the federal judge overseeing his case and requested a reduced sentence. The letter worked. Persuaded by Ray's argument, the judge reduced his sentence by six months, cutting it in half.

On December 3, 1946, Ray walked out of federal prison, fully convinced that the powers of hypnotism he developed through Voodoo had brought about his early release. With a renewed sense of purpose, he took a Greyhound bus to Astoria, New York, where he temporarily lived with his sister, Lena Cano, and found work in construction.

As Lena later recalled:

> He was always talking about some kind of spiritualism he learned about down there in Tallahassee from the others he was in prison with. He said they had a cult, something like Voodoo. They thought they could cast spells on people from a distance, especially if they could get a lock of hair or a photograph of some person. Raymond thought he could hypnotize from a distance too, and make anyone do just what he said – he could even kill that way if he wanted to.

A neighbor similarly remembered that Ray believed he could "make love to a woman from a distance. All he needed was a picture or a piece of clothing worn next to the skin. He said he could make any woman fall in love with him."

One evening after work, Ray noticed a copy of *Woman's Home House-keeper* magazine on his sister's coffee table. Bored and with nothing better to do, he picked the magazine up and began flipping through its pages. As he browsed through the articles in the magazine, one of the advertisements caught his eye: *Contact friends*, it urged, *Lonely Hearts*. The ad was from a correspondence club called Old Chelsea Station based out of New York City. It was just one of many such advertisements typical of the time that appeared in women's magazines and pulp publications, such as one from a club in Kansas City, Missouri:

> *Lonesome? Join Reliable Club, established 1909. Members everywhere – beautiful girls, nurses, teachers, widows, businessmen, farmers seeking congenial mates. Many claim wealth. Dignified, dependable and sure, we get results. Write for information and descriptions.*

Another from a club in Minneapolis, Minnesota read:

LONELY? Mail dollar bill – will send names and addresses of over
200 members of the opposite sex and list you in our club. Write us a
letter giving age, height, weight, with good description of yourself and
kind of mate desired.

An idea slowly crept into Ray's mind. He pictured himself living a
pampered, epicurean lifestyle, using funds fleeced from admiring
women to indulge his every whim and taste.

Invigorated by the prospect of easy money, Ray wrote to Old
Chelsea Station and requested more information. When he received a
response and application, he quickly filled it out and mailed the application back along with a $2 fee. Shortly after submitting the applica-
tion, Ray received four typed pages of paper containing an
alphabetized list of three to four hundred women's names and descriptions, including personal information such as their age, height, weight,
eye color, hair color, and hobbies. For most of the women, the list also
included their financial status and identified them as either a divorcee
or widow. Excited by the potential of his plan, Ray soon joined other
clubs too, reaching out to all of the women who interested him.

After tracking down a typewriter, Ray put his plan into action,
spending several nights sequestered in his room feverishly writing
letters. It did not take long for his efforts to bear fruit. Lonely women
from Mother Dinene's Friendly Club and the May Richardson Agency
in New York, and the Standard Correspondence Club of Illinois, wrote
back to him in droves. Using those three Lonely Hearts clubs, he eventually compiled a list of 205 prospective women who matched what he
was looking for: first and foremost they had promising finances.

While the women took the correspondence seriously, Ray treated it
as a mix of entertainment and a means to an end. Indeed, he often took
the letters to a local poolroom that served as a club for the Spanish men
in the neighborhood, where he read the letters aloud to amuse the
other men.

In the midst of his letter writing campaign, Ray began bouncing
from one job to the next. Though he had previously been a reliable and
hard-working employee, now he could not hold a job for more than a

few weeks. Instead, he spent hours in his room crafting correspondence aimed at charming his female admirers. He preferred women with exotic names like Mercedes, Portia, and Arabella, and he followed the same pattern with all of his pen pals. After he became sufficiently familiar with one of them through the exchange of several letters, he requested that she send him a photograph and a lock of her hair. Once he had these tokens in his possession, he would make a miniature figure or doll that served as a symbol of the woman who sent them. Using incense obtained from a Jamaican magic shop in Harlem, he placed the doll under a hypnotic spell that he believed would beguile the actual woman represented by the figure. And his Voodoo method brought a high rate of success; most of the women he selected eagerly agreed to meet him. Using his powerful animal magnetism, he had little trouble seducing them over the course of a few days. Inevitably, having fleeced what he wanted from his current conquest, he left her behind for his next unsuspecting victim.

In January 1947, Ray began corresponding with Jane Wilson Thompson, a 40-year-old dietician at Presbyterian Hospital who lived with her mother in a six-room apartment on West 139th Street in New York. He learned all about her, including that she had grown up in Corry, Pennsylvania, and attended Indiana State Teachers College before moving to New York and getting married.

Less than a week later, Ray met Jane in person. On their first date, they attended a church service together and then spent the rest of the day downtown at the Central Park Zoo. Ray wanted to present a wholesome appearance to the target of his newest con and in that endeavor he wholly succeeded. After a few weeks of dating, Ray moved into Jane's apartment. Throughout his romance of Jane, Ray was planning a trip back to Spain to see his wife and children. And in the not too distant future, Martha Beck awaited.

Chapter Three

O n April Fool's Day, the irony of which she could not help but notice, Martha Beck received several letters from male suitors who had seen her lonely hearts club profile. Out of the small handful of correspondence, one reply particularly piqued her interest:

Dear Martha,

I hope you'll allow me the liberty of addressing you by your Christian name. To tell the truth I don't quite know how to begin this letter to you because, I must confess, this is the first letter of this sort I have ever written.

Would you like to know a little about me? I'm thirty-four and I've been told I'm not a bad looking fellow. I am employed at the T & T Construction Company and I live with my sister's family in Astoria, New York.

Why did I choose you for my debut friendship letter? Because you are a nurse and therefore I know you have a full heart with a great capacity for comfort and love. I am hoping to find someone like you to build a life with and share my home.

Enclosed is a small snapshot of me. You can hopefully see from

this the type of person I am. If you would enjoy corresponding with
me, I'd be happy to do so with you.
    Your friend,
    Charles Raymond Fernandez

Ray had come across Martha's name in the newest mailing from Mother Dinene's Friendly Club. He liked that she was younger than most of the women on the listing. However, it was her name that had really captured his attention. Her middle name, Seabrook, instantly brought to mind William Seabrook, the author of *Magic Island*, the book about Voodoo that had so influenced him.

Enamored by Ray's letter, and perhaps captivated by his Voodoo charms, Martha wasted no time writing him back. She received several letters a week from him, and she answered every one in turn. The letters soon grew longer and the friendly conversational tone of their correspondence quickly shifted to something more romantic. They discussed their interests, shared their dreams, and exchanged photos of their families. Ray also started sending cards to Martha's daughter, signing them from her "New York Daddy."

After several months of correspondence, Ray proposed that they should get married. He disclosed that he had been drawn to her by a psychic power, and he believed their souls were fated to be together. Martha was so flattered by the focused attention and affection that she came to believe he was right.

In early September, Ray wrote that he would soon be going to Spain, but promised he would come visit her in Pensacola after he returned.

On September 18, Ray sailed for Spain on the *Pero de Alenquer*. Jane Thompson went with him. Registered for the voyage as husband and wife, the couple enjoyed the ship's stops at various ports along the route before reaching its final destination, Granada, on October 10. From there they visited Madrid, Malaga, and La Linea on the borderline of Gibraltar, with Jane happily paying all of their expenses.

In early November, Ray and Jane checked into the Hotel Sevilla in La Linea. Unbeknownst to Jane, Ray's wife, Encarnacion, lived with their four children in the Hotel Principe Alfonso in a nearby part of town. The next day, while Ray was attending to some business in Seville, Encarnacion came to the Hotel Sevilla looking for him. Instead, she found Jane. When Ray returned from his business affairs, he easily defused the potentially explosive situation, smoothing things over with his usual charm, and for the next few days the three spent most of their time together.

But on the night of November 7, Ray and Jane had a heated argument. Perhaps Jane learned the true nature of Ray's relationship with Encarnacion, or perhaps, having taken everything he needed from Jane, Ray provoked the argument on purpose with the intent of ending their relationship. Whatever the reason, Ray stormed out of the Hotel Sevilla and spent the night with Encarnacion. The next morning, a hotel maid found Jane dead in the room she had been sharing with Ray. After examining Jane's body, a local physician issued a death certificate attributing her sudden demise to "cardiacal collapse during acute gastro-enteritis." Ray hastily arranged for her burial in a La Linea cemetery.

Ray would later claim that Jane had been sick for two weeks with diarrhea and constipation before dying on November 7 with "stomach trouble and then heart trouble." Upon investigating the matter further, Spanish authorities learned that two days before Jane's death, Ray had visited the hotel pharmacy and purchased a bottle of digitalis, a medication used to treat heart conditions, which was known to be toxic even in small doses. Vomiting, nausea, diarrhea, and confusion were common signs of digitalis poisoning. Police found the bottle of digitalis in Jane's medicine closet with half of the contents missing, and the doctor who certified her death concluded that such an amount could have killed her. Based on the new information, Spanish authorities issued a warrant for Ray's arrest in connection with Jane's death. But he was long gone by then.

On November 29, Ray sailed for New York on the SS *Saturnia*. When he arrived back in New York on December 8, he somberly broke the news of Jane's death to her elderly mother, Pearl Wilson. After informing Pearl that her daughter had died of "heart failure" in Spain, Ray produced a copy of Jane's will, explaining that she signed it shortly before her death, bequeathing her apartment and all of its contents to him. Playing the role of a true gentleman, he assured Pearl that she could keep living in the apartment since he knew that is what Jane would have wanted. The grieving but grateful Mrs. Wilson had no idea that the story about Jane's death subsequently changed with Ray telling Jane's neighbors that she had died in a train accident.

After settling back into the apartment, Ray turned his attention back to the lonely hearts clubs, once again cranking out letters to financially attractive prospects, picking up where he left off before the trip to Spain. And meeting Martha Beck was now at the top of his list. A few days before Christmas, he telegrammed Martha proclaiming that he could not bear waiting any longer to see her.

Chapter Four

It was two weeks before Christmas and Martha felt like a kid waiting for Santa. She could not contain her excitement as she stood at the platform of the Pensacola train station, and the arrival of her mail-order Romeo did nothing to diminish that enthusiasm. Though "of slight build" and not a physically imposing figure, he carried himself with confidence, like a man of considerable stature. Standing 5'8" and weighing about 160 pounds, Ray's dark, slicked-back hair, "piercing" deep-set brown eyes, deep voice, and brooding look bore a striking resemblance to her favorite actor, Charles Boyer.

Even his "catlike walk" and slow, deliberate movements mimicked those of the French-American actor who rose to Hollywood prominence during the 1930's in romantic dramas such as *The Garden of Allah* (1936), *Algiers* (1938), and *Love Affair* (1939). More recently, Boyer's performance in *Gaslight*, the 1944 film in which he starred alongside Ingrid Bergman, had enthralled Martha with his hypnotic voice and dead-pan acting style. Little did she know that soon her life would in some ways mirror the movie advertised as the "strange story of an international criminal's love" and the "strange drama of a captive sweetheart." But when she saw Ray step off the train, it seemed to

Martha that Charles Boyer himself had stepped off the silver screen to stand before her in flesh and blood. Christmas appeared to have come early for Martha Beck.

Years later, an investigator who interviewed Ray would be struck by the resemblance to the famous actor as well, noting that he had "some of Boyer's animal force that seems to draw women to him, a natural hypnotic quality that repels men but fascinates women. His voice was deep and slow and all his movements deliberate. You got a sense of latent passion in him." The animal magnetism he projected left the contradictory impression of a wild but timid temperament.

After exchanging nervous pleasantries and getting over the jitters of finally meeting face-to-face, Martha drove Ray to her apartment, eager to impress him with her cooking skill and anxious to introduce him to her two children. She worried about how he would react to the children and was relieved to see that Ray greeted them warmly and even spent an hour playing with them by the Christmas tree. The next two days went by in the blink of an eye. Ray asked Martha if, now that she had met him, she was "willing to take a chance" and marry him. She was, and they made plans to marry in Mobile, Alabama. However, on the day they were supposed to go to Mobile, Ray told her that he needed to return to New York to take care of some business. Despite her pleas to stay longer, he insisted that he must go. Wiping the tears from her cheeks, Ray promised Martha that he would come back to her or send money so she could join him in New York.

Over the next few days, Martha wrote Ray long letters professing her undying love for him. On December 23, the day Ray was supposed to come back to her in Pensacola, Martha received a letter from him. Ray wrote in an apologetic tone that "he was afraid that he had made a mistake and that it would be best for [her] to remain in Pensacola with [her] job and two children."

Martha was devastated. She had felt a connection to Ray that she had never experienced before. She felt more alive for those few days of his visit than she had for as long as she could remember. Now heartbroken, she was confused and frightened and unsure about what to do. She knew one thing though. She did not want to go back to the way things were before she met Ray, to the dreary, disappointed life that always left her feeling empty inside.

Around 9:00 p.m. on December 26, Martha put her two children to bed, closed all of the windows, and turned on all of the gas jets in the apartment. Fumes faintly hissed as they flowed from all four burners of the stove, the oven, and the gas heater. As the gas filled the apartment, she wrote Ray a letter stating that if he could not be a part of her life, she would rather not live at all. But Fate again intervened. As Martha began getting light-headed, Dorothy Lynn rushed through the door. Dorothy, her friend and neighbor, had smelled the gas outside. Quickly grasping the gravity of the situation, she shut off the heater, stove, and oven, and opened the windows to air out the apartment. After checking on the children, she listened to Martha's explanation. Touched by her friend's desperation, Dorothy mailed Martha's suicide letter to Ray along with a cover letter explaining that she found it in the apartment and was sending it to him without Martha's knowledge.

The letter frightened Ray. Aside from any personal feelings he might have had for Martha, he worried about what could happen if she succeeded in killing herself: he might find himself squarely in the cross-hairs of a police investigation. That was attention he had no intention of attracting. He quickly telephoned Martha to "get that foolish or crazy idea out of her mind about suicide." Dorothy answered the phone and told him that Martha was in bed "sick from the fumes of gas," too sick to come to the phone. When Ray called again the next day, Martha was well enough to talk to him. He invited her to come visit him in New York for a week or two. She accepted without any hesitation and took a two-week leave of absence from her job at the Crippled Children's Home, packed her bags, and booked a trip north.

On January 2, 1948, Martha arrived at Pennsylvania Station in New York City. In a role reversal from their first meeting in Florida, Ray was waiting for her at the platform.

"You're a crazy little fool, aren't you," Ray said, greeting her with a half-grin before taking her to his apartment at 505 West 139th Street. After settling in to Apartment 44, the conversation soon turned to Martha's suicide attempt.

"If you're ever going to do something like that again, be thoughtful enough not to involve your kids," Ray admonished her. "Don't have the kids around when you turn on the jets."

Martha studied his face and frowned.

"If I go, I want my children to go with me," she said in all seriousness.

If her response surprised Ray, he did not show it. Instead, he seemed strangely pleased by the intensity of her sentiments.

Later that night, Ray decided three people in the apartment was a crowd. Pearl Wilson would have to leave. Casting it as a better situation for her, he told Pearl to make arrangements to stay with her son in Wilmington, North Carolina. Not long after that, he and Martha took Pearl to the train station and saw her off.

Over the next ten days, Ray and Martha enjoyed each other's company, going to dinner clubs and taking in shows. Martha thought they were growing closer, but the night before she left, Ray told her that although he loved her, he already had a wife and four kids in Spain.

"You need to go home to Pensacola and forget about me," he said flatly.

Martha teared up.

"Do you really think it's possible to forget someone after you've grown attached to them?" she asked with desperation in her voice. "Do you think I can just forget you like erasing words on a sheet of paper?"

Although she had never imagined meeting someone like Ray before, now that she had, she could not imagine losing him. Ray's treatment of her – his kindness and thoughtfulness – was something she had never known before. She always had his complete attention and he "practically waited on her hand and foot," always helping with cleaning the apartment and cooking. Moreover, he was "very lovable," happily taking her to the movies, dancing, and dinner. In Martha's mind, Ray was "all that a woman could ask for in a man." So when Ray said they could not be together anymore, the ground might as well have opened up and swallowed her. Despite Martha's pleas to stay with him, Ray escorted her to the train station and sent her on her way. But in her heart she knew they would not be apart for long.

On her first day back at work, Martha was summoned to the head administrator's office and summarily discharged as Superintendent of the Crippled Children's Home. Although surprised by the sudden termination, Martha's only concern was Ray. He was the only thing that mattered. She took the sudden firing as a sign that justified in her head what her heart already knew to be true. She cashed her final paycheck and caught the next bus back to New York City.

Ray was not amused when Martha called on January 19 and surprised him with the news that she was at Penn Station with her son and daughter. And yet, despite his annoyance about her unannounced visit, he volunteered to pick her up at a hotel near the train station. His initial anger subsided after Martha explained that she had lost her job and had nowhere else to go. Seeing how affectionate Ray acted towards her and the kids after learning about their situation cemented in Martha's mind that she would always love him.

However, the next day, Ray gave her an ultimatum. She could stay with him, but the children would have to go.

"I don't know how much longer I can take this," he told her. "If you were alone, you could stay with me as long as we live, but I am not going to be able to take the children too."

Torn between a mother's natural love for her children and the romantic love of her passion for what she believed to be the perfect man, she decided that if the children were the only thing blocking her new life with Ray then she would find another home for them. The thought of losing her children hurt her heart, but the thought of losing Ray threatened to destroy it.

> At that time I was torn between two loves, the love for my two children and my love for Mr. Fernandez. I weighed the two and I knew that I had no place to go with the children; I had no one to turn to. The day that I had left Pensacola my mother had gone to the station with me and she told me if I left I was no longer her daughter; that she never wanted to see or hear of me again, and I knew Mr. Fernandez did love me and that I loved him.

The next day she took her young son and daughter to Penn Station Traveler's Aid to ask about placing them for adoption. Told that the process would likely take weeks, she changed plans and took the children to a Salvation Army shelter instead. Pretending that they were all spending the night, she watched her son go to sleep and then noticed her daughter still awake.

"Keep an eye on your brother," Martha told her with a forced smile. "I'm going out to buy some candy." She tiptoed to the door, waved a silent goodbye, and walked out, never saw her children again.

As Martha hurried from the shelter to the subway station, the reality of what she was doing began sinking in. Her chest started hurting and she suddenly felt dizzy. The siren song of suicide called to her once again; an impulse came over her to end it all.

"I always felt like destroying myself would be the right thing to do," she explained.

She felt an irresistible force pulling her towards the subway tracks. She stepped to the edge of the track and waited, staring intently at the light of an approaching train. As the train sped toward her, she took a step forward. Suddenly someone grabbed her arm and yanked her back.

"Don't get too close to the track," a policeman warned her while still holding her arm. "The suction of the train might pull you over the edge."

For a few seconds, she stared at him in a daze. Then she blankly thanked him and stumbled out of the station, thinking only of making her way back to Ray.

Chapter Five

The next few weeks were a "deliriously happy" time in Martha's life. She and Ray went to movies together, went dancing, went out to dinner, and enjoyed sightseeing. Ray was "kind, considerate, thoughtful, and practically waited on [her] hand and foot." The way Ray treated her was "something [s]he had never had before." Every Saturday night, they stayed at a hotel downtown close to their favorite theater. The two were inseparable.

"No matter what room I was in, Raymond was always along with me," she told the jury. "He was very lovable. He was caressing me quite often. It was just about all that a woman could ask for in a man....I was very much in love with him and I still am."

On several occasions, Ray took her to one of his favorite spots, Sammie's Bowery Follies, a bar and nightclub featuring ex-vaudeville stars and former dancers, most of them considerably overweight and nearly all over sixty years old, suggesting that Ray had developed an unusual taste in women after his head injury.

Martha's devotion to him and sacrifice by choosing him over her children made a big impression on Ray, so much so that he decided to come clean to her. Now he understood how powerful an influence he had over her, and he knew that she would do anything for him. He soon felt comfortable enough to tell her about his "line of business" scamming women he met through lonely hearts clubs. He even shared the name of his current correspondent: Esther Henne, a school teacher from Laureldale, Pennsylvania, a suburb of Reading.

Unfazed by Ray's revelations, Martha pledged to him that those faked romances paled in comparison to the love they shared. To demonstrate the depth of her devotion to him, Martha assured Ray that if he ever found another woman he truly loved, she would leave him alone, but she promised that until that day came she would stay by his side. Martha's pledge of unwavering loyalty pleased Ray, stoking his ego while affirming his self-image of a modern-day Casanova.

"Don't be silly," he told her with a sly smile, "no matter how many women I meet, you're the only one that I love or will ever love."

Those were words Martha longed to hear, but they did not entirely eliminate her self-doubt.

"Do you think you could be happy with another woman?" she asked timidly.

Ray chuckled softy and flashed a devilish grin.

"I don't know, maybe I could," he admitted before quickly adding, "but if I can marry another woman and take her money, I can send it to Spain and get a divorce. Then you and I can get married and have a chance at real happiness."

Martha brightened at the thought of them sharing a future together, but Ray insisted on one rule for their relationship: if Martha stayed with him, she could not interfere with his scams.

"I love you and you can stay with me if you want, but you are not going to lead my life," Ray warned. "Anything that I want to do, I am going to do it, whether you approve of it or not."

Martha did not bat an eye. She would have agreed to anything to be with him.

"Of course, darling," Martha purred, trying not to notice the twinge of jealousy already fluttering in her heart.

The day before Valentine's Day, Ray boarded a train bound for Reading, Pennsylvania. His ardent letters to Esther Henne had achieved their goal. Now he was going to meet her. Martha remained at the apartment in New York, "very much hurt and upset" to be left behind. She tried to talk him out of going, but he would not be swayed. However, before he left, he pledged his devotion to her.

"No matter how many women I meet, no matter how many women I write to, you are the only woman that I love or will ever love," he promised her.

Like many other women before her, Esther felt an immediate attraction upon meeting Ray. She was drawn to his deep-set eyes and swarthy hair. His words and body language projected a caring and attentive personality, while his eyes hinted at something dark concealed underneath. Paired with his genteel manner was a bad-boy attitude that women found attractive without even realizing it. There was something exotic about him that gave rise to a peculiar charm, a hypnotic power that overcame any instinctual wariness and convinced women to trust him.

Although the beginning of their relationship was in fact very recent, Esther felt as if she had known Ray for much of her life. What began as paper pronouncements of romance soon transformed into talk of marriage. After the initial two-day stay in Reading, Ray went back to New York with plans to return to Esther by the end of the month to get married.

On February 28, this time with Martha in tow, Ray took a train back to Reading where Esther eagerly awaited. Ray introduced Martha to her as his step-sister, and the three drove all night to Fairfax, Virginia. In a bare-bones ceremony administered by the Clerk of the Court, Ray and Esther exchanged vows in the courthouse. Martha stood beside Ray as an official witness to the ceremony, the happy expression on her face giving no hint of the simmering resentment in her heart.

"It was all I could do to keep from screaming that he should not marry that woman when he was in love with me," Martha testified.

After the simple ceremony, the three drove back to Laureldale so

Esther could freshen up and retrieve some clothes before moving into Ray's apartment in New York. While Esther enjoyed a bath, her first as Mrs. Fernandez, Martha led Ray into the bedroom eager to release the sexual tension that had been building between them. Their discreet moment of passion was intense but short-lived and over by the time Esther finished her bath and dressed, humming to herself happily, oblivious to the true nature of Ray and Martha's relationship.

Esther's newlywed bliss did not last for long. Without her knowledge, Martha pawned some of Esther's jewelry using the name "Shelia Mason" to cover her tracks, and on March 2 Esther noticed that her money belt stuffed with $500 cash was missing. After frantically searching throughout the apartment that night, she found the belt – emptied of the $500 – in Martha's dresser drawer. Although Martha proclaimed her innocence, denying any knowledge about how the empty money belt ended up in her drawer, the seeds of suspicion were firmly planted.

Meanwhile, Ray continued to schmooze and pamper Esther hoping to persuade her to sign over her insurance policies and teacher's pension fund to him. But when his efforts failed to bear fruit after several days, his personality abruptly changed. It was a scene out of Gaslight where Charles Boyer's character changed "from a suave, debonair gentleman to a cunning, fiendish villain." Where he had been kind, considerate, and sweet, Ray now became irritable, prone to angry outbursts, and verbally abusive.

Confused by the sudden personality change and intimidated by Ray's aggressive behavior, Esther began to give in to his demands. It started with transferring registration of her car to him and giving him $500 to pay rent. Then on March 4, Esther accompanied Martha to a local bank, having agreed to sign her insurance policies over to Ray. But as they approached the street corner of the bank's location, Esther had second thoughts. Ignoring Martha's pleas, she dashed away from the bank and managed to lose Martha at the railroad station. When she returned to Ray's apartment, Esther spotted her car parked outside on the street. Realizing that she had been duped by her Spanish Romeo and his accomplice, Esther jumped in the car and drove back to her family in Laureldale, highly upset but relieved to be free of the pair's deception and influence. After returning home, she found receipts from a pawn shop in the glove compartment of her car. They were all that remained of the jewelry Martha had pawned using the name "Shelia Mason."

Spooked by Esther's getaway, Ray sold the apartment he had appropriated from Jane Thompson, pocketing $1500 from the sale. Empowered by the infusion of cash, Ray took Martha on a trip to Miami, Florida and Havana, Cuba during the first week of May. After the subtropical vacation, they decided to relocate to Chicago. Ray found work as a mechanic for the Western Dry Color Company and Martha took a job as a registered nurse in the obstetrical department of St. Luke's Hospital. On May 17, they moved into their new apartment, an upstairs unit at 5927 South Washtenaw Avenue.

While Ray and Martha settled into their new life in Chicago, the effects of a decade and a half of depression and war still oppressed many Americans. Although the end of World War II a few years earlier started an economic recovery that eventually grew strong, the ripples of positive impact took too long to reach lower class Americans like the Chalifoux family in Chicago. Forty-year-old Ray Chalifoux and his twenty-four-year-old wife, Lucille, had four young children to feed and a fifth on the way when Ray lost his job as a coal truck driver. Facing eviction from their apartment and the very real possibility of being homeless, Ray and Lucille were driven to desperate measures to survive. On August 4, 1948, they posted a sign in front of their apartment, reading: *4 CHILDREN FOR SALE Inquire Within*. A newspaper article published the next day with a photograph of the children and sign led to an outpouring of assistance for the family. But Lucille eventually did the unthinkable, selling her five-year-old daughter, RaeAnn, and four-year-old son, Milton, to complete strangers for the sum of $2.00. The buyers, John and Ruth Zoeteman, forced the children to work as slave labor on their farm, regularly keeping them tied-up in the barn when they were not toiling in the fields.

With the money from the sale of Jane Thompson's apartment nearly gone, Ray went back to the Lonely Hearts well. This time he set his sights on 40-year-old Myrtle Young from Green Forest, Arkansas. The $6000 in savings she had listed on her club profile made her an attractive option to the once again cash-poor Casanova. After exchanging several lengthy letters with Myrtle under the guise of "Charles Martin," Ray took a Greyhound bus to Springfield, Missouri, where she was visiting her daughter. Ray arrived in the afternoon and they spent the rest of the day getting better acquainted. Like a predator stalking its prey, Ray seized on Myrtle's vulnerability, sensing her loneliness and feeding on her need to be loved. Some people claim an ability to sense the presence of evil, but Myrtle never sensed that Ray represented a threat. That night they went to an amusement park that reminded Ray of Coney Island. As they sat and watched the colorful carousel turn around and around, they made plans for Myrtle to come to Chicago.

On August 12, Ray picked up Myrtle at the Greyhound bus station in Chicago. Careful to maintain the ruse, Ray introduced Martha to Myrtle as his "sister" and then took her to the South Washtenaw Avenue apartment that he and Martha shared. Myrtle shared one of the two bedrooms with Martha, while Ray slept in the other bedroom. Like Jane Thompson and Esther Henne, Myrtle fell for Ray's dark charm, mesmerized by what she mistook for the passion of true romance. Two days later, Myrtle married "Charles Martin" in a civil ceremony in Chicago as Martha looked on resentfully.

Martha's jealousy was shared by Myrtle. Each wanted Ray solely for herself. Each wanted the other woman gone. Shortly after the wedding, Myrtle wired her bank in Green Forest, Arkansas, directing that her life savings be transferred to a joint account at the First

National Bank in Chicago. She named "Charles" as joint owner of the account before withdrawing $2000 and spending it to buy him a car. That evening, Myrtle footed the bill for a fancy dinner and movie for her new husband and his ever-present sister.

Myrtle felt the time was right to get rid of Martha.

"Don't you think the apartment is a little small for three people?" she asked Ray when Martha was out of ear shot. "Can't you ask Martha to find a room someplace else?"

Though he agreed the apartment was too small for the three of them, Ray did not answer her. He had already decided on different course of action. Now that he had swindled another love-sick suitor, Ray gave Martha the go ahead to get rid of her. Later that night, Martha slipped Myrtle a heavy dose of barbiturates that quickly caused her to lose consciousness.

Just what else Martha did to Myrtle that night is unclear; however, early the next morning, Ray helped Martha put Myrtle on a bus headed for Little Rock, Arkansas. From there they hurried to the First National Bank where they emptied the joint account Myrtle had opened just the day before. Then Ray and Martha left town. Over the next two weeks, they traveled to towns in Tennessee, North Carolina, and South Carolina to wine and dine women Ray had met through lonely hearts clubs. They spent a couple of days with one of the women, Lela Smith of Memphis, Tennessee, but ultimately none of them had enough financial resources to merit more than fleeting attention.

On August 18, as Ray and Martha continued their tour scamming unsuspecting women, a bus driver discovered Myrtle Young, dazed and barely coherent, slumped against the back seat of a bus in Springfield, Missouri. Unable to walk on her own, Myrtle had to be carried off. Fellow passengers reported hearing her muttering something about having been held captive in Chicago until she surrendered her money. After being notified of her whereabouts, Myrtle's confused family had her transported to the State Hospital in Little Rock, Arkansas. A week later, she died there of "heart disease" without giving a coherent account of what had happened to her. The doctors who treated her there suspected that she suffered a cerebral hemorrhage a week or two before her death, a condition which would have been consistent with being beaten or otherwise struck in her head. Myrtle was buried in Callens Branch Cemetery in her hometown of Green Forest, Arkansas.

All the while, whenever possible and at least every few weeks, Ray sent money by Western Union to his wife and children in Spain. The amount varied, but by having a man in Gibraltar convert the dollars into pounds, Ray ensured that Encarnacion and his kids were able to live a comfortable life.

Chapter Six

Having little success during their road trip and running low on funds, Ray and Martha returned to the familiar surroundings of New York, but they were not idle for long. Ray decided to pay a surprise visit to his newest lonely hearts correspondent, Irene De la Point, who he had been exchanging amorous letters with under the guise of "Charles Martin." On August 30, the pair drove to Springfield, Vermont to meet her.

"I hope she's another hag," Martha grumbled during the drive, already upset about Ray courting another woman.

"She isn't," Ray remarked, amused by Martha's jealousy. "She's 39, blonde, and sounds quite attractive.

The car was quiet for some moments as Martha stared out the window.

"Martha, remember your promise not to interfere," Ray added. "Why don't you go back to Florida for a while and let me be?"

She turned from the window and faced Ray.

"You're the only man who can make me happy," she said. "I'll never let you go."

The look in her eyes told him that she meant it, but he let the comment go unanswered and returned his gaze to the horizon of the road ahead.

When they arrived at Irene's house, "Charles Martin" introduced Martha to her as his sister using their standard ruse. Irene was as attractive as Ray had hoped. Excited by her beauty compared to most of his lonely heart's lovers, he stayed with Irene for several weeks, while Martha slept at a boarding house nearby not bothering to hide her resentment of Ray's latest companion. Typical of his technique, Ray eventually steered his conversations with Irene to marriage, a topic to which she was readily agreeable. Indeed, before long they drove to Burlington, Vermont to get premarital blood tests.

When they returned from Burlington, Martha joined them for dinner and noticed a spot of blood on Ray's shirt sleeve.

"What's that?" she asked, pointing it out to him. "Did you hurt yourself?"

Ray glanced down at his sleeve with mild surprise.

"Oh, that's nothing," he laughed. "We just had some blood tests done."

"For what?" Martha pressed, clearly growing agitated.

"Charles and I are going to get married!" Irene announced with the excitement of the newly engaged.

Martha tried to put on a happy face, but this was news to her, and unwelcomed news at that.

"Oh," was all she managed to say.

The negative tone of her reaction puzzled Irene.

"What's wrong?" Irene asked with a look of concern.

"I can't tell you," Martha replied, trying to stifle her emotions.

Irene's eyes narrowed. Something began to dawn on her.

"If I didn't know better," she remarked, "I'd say there's more love between you and Charles than the ordinary brother-sister kind."

"Don't be silly!" Martha exclaimed. She did her best to put on a happy face, but managed only a faint smile.

"I love my brother and hearing he's getting married surprised me is all. I'm happy for you both, I really am."

Her apparent sincerity satisfied Irene, yet the façade of happiness did nothing to extinguish the jealousy still smoldering in Martha's heart. Over the next few days, it intensified and spread until she felt she must do something or her heart would explode. She suspected that Ray was not just pretending anymore, that he had really fallen in love with Irene. Unable to contain her simmering emotions, Martha vented them by taking a page from Ray's playbook: she would write a letter to Irene revealing the truth of her relationship. Just as Irene's lonely hearts club letter of introduction set events in motion that threatened to take Ray away from her, Martha's letter would turn back the clock and reclaim him.

In a three-page letter to Irene, Martha exposed Ray's true motives. *The gentleman that has posed as my brother is not my brother*, Martha wrote. *He is my sweetheart and I've been living with him for quite some time as his wife.* The letter revealed that "Charles's" real name was Raymond Fernandez, that he was married to a woman in Spain, and he had married several women in the recent past including Esther Henne of Laureldale, Pennsylvania, and Myrtle Young in Chicago. The letter continued: *You should know that if he marries you it will be for your money and not out of any love for you.* After implying that Irene would end up like Myrtle Young, Martha concluded the letter by directing much of her spite at Ray, asking Irene: *Will you please call the police and put him in jail?*

Unaware of Martha's unleashed rancor, Ray thought everything was going according to plan. He was wholly pleased with the situation until he received a letter from Irene that not only abruptly cancelled their intended marriage, but also broke off their relationship entirely. She told him that she could no longer trust him after reading Martha's letter.

Enraged by Martha's meddling, Ray immediately confronted her.

"Are you crazy?" he shouted, smacking her across the face with the back of his open hand. "You've destroyed everything I worked for."

"I don't care," Martha told him with tears running down her cheeks. "I would rather see you in jail than with another woman."

She feared Ray's dark side, yet she also found it somehow alluring. Any attention from him was better than being ignored; being hit was better than no attention at all. Ray jerked his hand back to strike her again, then stopped himself and took a few steps away.

"Your jealousy is out of control," he said regaining his composure. "I can't put up with it anymore." The anger was gone from his voice, replaced by its normal, measured tone. "We need to end this," he said solemnly. "You go your way and I'll go mine."

Martha stared at him in shock as he turned and walked away.

Still hoping to salvage the situation, Ray wrote an apologetic letter to Irene explaining that it was all a misunderstanding and asking for another chance. It did not take long for her reply to arrive:

I only wish I had a way of looking down deep into your heart and reading what is there. True, as you say, there would always be doubt between us after those hideous things Martha has told me. She even implied you intended to do away with me, as you did with Jane, after you succeeded in getting what I had. Then you could go away and enjoy yourself with her, your only true love.

Though he projected a calm demeanor on the outside, in his mind Ray still raged at Martha for her jealous interference. Fed up with her possessiveness, Ray informed her in no uncertain terms that she would have to move out of the apartment and to pack her things because he was going to the bus station to get her a one-way ticket to go stay with her sister in South Carolina.

When Ray returned from the bus station, he found Martha sitting on the bed with a .22 rifle pointed at her chest. Her eyes were red from crying.

"I'm going to pull the trigger if you don't promise me I can stay with you," she sobbed.

Ray walked over to the bed and gently sat down beside her.

"Honey, let's talk about it," he cooed, trying to calm her. "You know I only love you."

"You're just saying that try to stop me!" she bawled while lowering the gun barrel slightly.

"No, I mean it," Ray promised while looking tenderly into her eyes. "I've always loved you."

His proclamations of love slowly began to calm her and when he saw her grip on the gun loosen slightly, he snatched it away from her.

"You really are crazy!" Ray screamed as he stood up from the bed.

"I'm sorry...I'm sorry," Martha stammered through more tears.

But Ray was not listening as he gathered up her bags. He would not let her emotions endanger the livelihood he had worked so hard to establish. Whatever feelings he had for her were not worth abandoning his rightful lifestyle. With barely another word, he drove Martha to the Greyhound station, put her on a bus bound for Woodruff, South Carolina, and watched from the loading area as the bus pulled away.

Less than a week later, a letter from Martha arrived. She begged him to take her back, writing that she was several months pregnant, and pleading with him to think about their unborn child. Several weeks later, Ray called her. He had changed his mind.

"I didn't realize how much I loved you until we were apart," he told her.

To Martha, Ray's words meant a new lease on life. The prospect of being back by his side instantly swept the shadows of despair from her mind, transforming her outlook to pure joy despite the fact that Ray also stressed that she should abort her pregnancy if she wanted to come back to him. After all, getting rid of an unborn fetus would be easier than abandoning her son and daughter had been. Once again, what Ray wanted, he got. Eager to please him, Martha tried several different means of bringing about a miscarriage before finding one that worked by sticking a crochet needle up into her vagina to puncture her uterus. The immediate result of the self-induced procedure was a watery discharge, but she felt confident it would eventually bring about the wanted miscarriage.

The next day, she caught a ride to Spartansburg, where she pawned her watch to buy a bus ticket so she could return to Ray. Around the same time across the Atlantic, Spanish authorities issued a warrant for Ray's arrest in connection with the suspicious death of Jane Thompson.

On November 2, 1948, Harry S. Truman won a stunning Presidential election, rallying from behind to overcome what had seemed an unsurmountable lead and defeat New York Governor Thomas E. Dewey. Having gone to print with Dewey well ahead in the polls, headlines in national newspapers distributed for sale the next morning erroneously announced what they had quite reasonably presumed would be a Dewey victory. After the final votes were tallied, an exuberant Truman posed for photographs triumphantly holding a copy of the November 3 edition of the *Chicago Daily Tribune* with the faulty proclamation *Dewey Defeats Truman* in big, bold letters as the front-page headline.

Elected Governor of New York in 1942, Thomas Dewey had been the Republican candidate for President for the previous election in 1944 as well, but lost that bid for the Presidency to Franklin D. Roosevelt. But this second loss to Truman stung even more due to its immense improbability. Yet, in the not too distant future, Dewey would become an important figure in the lives of the Lonely Hearts Killers.

On the same day of the *Chicago Daily Tribune*'s erroneous headline, Martha Beck arrived by bus in New York City. Ray was waiting to welcome her and take her back to his apartment. She soon found a job as a nanny for a local family, where she worked despite feeling slightly ill from the risky procedure. She started having severe abdominal pains a few days later on November 7, and she went into labor while the family she worked for was away. Desperate and alone, she delivered a dead, but almost fully matured, baby girl on their bathroom floor, then wrapped it in a towel and threw it into the home's incinerator.

Meanwhile, Ray continued exchanging correspondence with women he met through the lonely hearts clubs, sometimes getting five or six letters a day. On December 7, he received a list of new members for one of the clubs he repeatedly used. Invoking his Voodoo powers of divination, one name stood out to him as a promising new target. She was a widow living nearby in Albany. Her name was Janet J. Fay.

Part Two

Love, now at last you've found me
Hold me and call me always
Thrill me and fill all my day
And weave your magic spell round me

"L'Amour Toujours L'Amour" – Catherine Cushing 1922

"The things we do for love" – Jamie Lannister, *Game of Thrones*

Chapter Seven

J anet Fay's profile on the lonely hearts club new member list stated that she was 41 years old, 5'4" tall, and weighed 135 pounds. The descriptive summary included that said she was "attractive" and "liked dancing," and most importantly for Ray, it disclosed that she had almost $7,000 in savings. The listing also conveyed the importance of her Christian faith. Like a predator honed in on its prey, Ray dispatched a letter to Janet introducing himself as "Charles Martin" and explaining that, like her, he was a Catholic with strong spiritual beliefs.

Recently widowed from a marriage over two decades long, Janet was lonely and very receptive to Ray's "gentlemanly" letter. She promptly penned a reply:

Dear Charles,

I was all excited to receive your sweet letter. It is so nice to write to someone who is such a good man and who has such a wonderful sister as you have.

The picture is lovely. Sometimes I wish I still had mine. When my husband died, Mary, my daughter, and her husband, Alton, were so kind and helped me to sell my house and belongings. The ten thousand dollars I got means that I can live quite comfortably alone in my hotel apartment. It is not very big, but I do not need too much space to do the things I have to do.

But I do miss the company of the late Mr. Fay. He was such a wonderful man....I must close now, dear Charles, or else I will be late for church. I will pray for you and your sister.

God bless you both,

Janet J. Fay

While Ray continued wooing Janet through the mail, he and Martha went house hunting. On December 17, using the names Mr. and Mrs. Charles Raymond Martin, they paid $200 for two-month's advance rent and moved into the upper floor apartment of a house at 15 Adeline Place in the Village of Valley Stream on Long Island. Their apartment occupied most of the top floor of the imitation brick, two-story house that had been converted to a two-family dwelling by the owners. The modest home had tar shingles and an open porch with a foyer leading to stairs that provided access to the second floor. The top of the stairs led directly into the kitchen. The diminutive apartment's one bedroom, one bathroom, and living room were all located to the right of the entrance. After placing a "For Rent" advertisement in the *Long Island Press*, the landlady, Mrs. Walter Arnsperger, happily accepted the "Martins" as tenants, finding them to be "quiet and pleasant." Ray and Martha quickly personalized the small space with a bookcase, clock, silver jewelry box, radio, two "expensive" cigarette cases, and several portraits of Ray's family on the walls.

On December 26, Ray picked up the mail at his sister's house, which he used as his permanent address due to his frequent relocations. Among his mail was a Christmas card from Irene De le Pointe and six letters from other lonely hearts club suitors, including the most recent one from Janet Fay.

Believing that any man as religious as "Charles" must be "good," Janet had invited him to come to Albany to meet her in person. Ray smiled as he read, pleased that his persuasive writing skills had once again paid off, this time after only three or four letters. He accepted

Janet's invitation without hesitation. After all, this was what he had been working toward.

His work day with the Tomisetti & Tomisetti Construction Company building a bridge for the Long Island Railroad had been cut short due to an increasingly heavy snow fall. Now he hurried home through the accumulating snow and surprised Martha with the news that they were going to drive to Albany.

"Get dressed, Martha," he announced as he came through the doorway.

"Why," Martha asked, startled by his sudden appearance.

"I want to meet Miss Fay."

The look on Martha's face instantly changed from one of pleasant surprise to that of sullen disappointment.

"I don't want you to go," she replied, trying to dissuade him. "Let's spend the rest of the holiday together, just you and me."

"Don't be silly," Ray scoffed, "according to her description this woman has four or five thousand dollars. I need to go meet her."

Realizing that Ray was going irrespective of her feelings about the matter, Martha reluctantly agreed to accompany him and, once again, pose as his sister. Her sense of self was now so centered around Ray that even though she did not want him to keep meeting women through the correspondence clubs, she would rather go with him than let him out of her sight.

On the morning of December 30, Ray and Martha drove to Albany. They arrived in town just before sunset and checked into the New Kenmore Hotel on Pearl Street, registering as Mr. and Mrs. Martinez Fernandez for a room on the top floor. They spent the night together and the next morning Ray left to meet Janet. After making the short, thirteen-block trip, Ray pulled his blue Pontiac into the driveway of Janet's apartment at 276 Hamilton Street. When she answered the door, Ray had to struggle to maintain his suave composure. The woman standing before him was obviously much older than the 41-years stated in her club profile. In truth, she was 66. But Ray had invested too much time and effort to abandon the plan at that point. He steadied himself, flashed Janet a smile, and employed his customary charm. He used the same approach every time, subtle blandishment, persuasion through flattery, a few kind words and gestures. It was a tried-and-true strategy for getting what he wanted from lonely women.

After some polite small-talk, Janet asked if they could pay a visit to a friend of hers, Ann Mason, who had submitted Janet's name to the lonely hearts club. Since Ann had put the wheels in motion that had brought them together, Janet wanted "Charles" to meet her. Still fully in charm mode, Ray readily agreed. Ever the Romeo, when Ray learned that Ann had recently separated from her husband, he remarked, "It's too bad I didn't meet you before. I would have married *you.*"

After leaving Ann Mason's home, Ray and Janet went to dinner and a movie, then returned to Janet's apartment. They talked about their faith and families, their hobbies, and other aspects of their lives. When Janet told him she would like to meet his family, Ray shared that his sister, Martha, was at their hotel, and promised to bring her to meet Janet the following day. Ray left at 10:00 p.m. and spent the rest of New Year's Eve with Martha. As bells and horns sounded in the streets below, they welcomed the new year by enjoying one another under the bed sheets of their hotel room.

On Saturday, the first day of the new year, Ray and Martha drove to Janet's apartment for breakfast. Ray/Charles introduced Janet to "Martha Martin," his sister, and the two of them seemed to hit it off from the start. To play on Janet's sympathies, Ray told her that his wallet had been stolen during New Year's Eve festivities and they would need to return to New York City since he was nearly out of cash. The story achieved its intended effect: Janet invited them to stay with her in her one-room, Murphy-style apartment. Later that afternoon the three of them drove around Albany sightseeing before going to a movie in Schenectady and having a late dinner at the Waldorf Café in Albany.

During dinner, Janet asked for details about Ray's job, what he did, how much money he made. When she seemed satisfied with his answers, Ray in turn asked Janet about her finances.

"My lawyer told me never to tell any men I meet about how much money I have or don't have," she said in a slightly embarrassed tone.

She told Ray that she had letters from other men interested in meeting her, but she had only wanted to meet him. Ray asked Janet if she wanted to see New York City. She did. The conversation turned to talk of marriage and having Janet move back to New York City with him. Afterward, they returned to Janet's apartment where, due to the tight quarters, Ray slept on the studio couch, while Janet and Martha shared the Murphy bed that pulled down from the wall on the other side of the room.

Unable to sleep, Janet sat by the couch talking to Ray until nearly 1:00 a.m., at times caressing Ray's face.

"What's the matter," she whispered, "don't you want to kiss me?"

"Janet, this isn't the time or place for that," Ray replied, tired but trying to be polite. "What if Martha wakes up?"

"She's sound asleep. I already checked."

Ray gently took her hand.

"I want to wait until after we're married to do anything like that," he replied doing his best imitation of a good Catholic gentleman.

Janet smiled and nodded approvingly before going back to bed. She loved that "Charles" actively practiced his Catholic creed, just like her deceased husband had incorporated his religious faith into his daily life. She slept soundly the rest of the night, her dreams aided by the belief that God had brought them together.

Chapter Eight

On Sunday, January 2, 1949, Ray and Martha attended Catholic mass with Janet at her parish church, the Cathedral of the Immaculate Conception near Albany's Mansion District. It was all part of the act. Janet needed to believe that Ray was a good, god-fearing Catholic. After church, they drove to Amsterdam, New York, about 15 miles from Albany, to visit Janet's step-daughter, Mary Spencer, and Mary's husband, Alton. In a scene similar to those that had played out before with Ray's previous conquests, Janet introduced him as Charles Martin and Martha as his sister.

When the sun began to set, Ray politely advised that they needed to get going because with nightfall, ice would form on the roads back to Janet's apartment in Albany. As they made their way home, Janet shared with Ray that Mary and Alton both liked him and had voiced their approval of him to her. Reassured by her family's endorsement, Janet became receptive to Ray's suggestions about her finances. She agreed to go with him the next morning to withdraw all of her money from the three banks where she had savings accounts.

As the three spent more time together, Janet began to feel like there was something a little odd about Ray and Martha's relationship. She could not quite put her finger on it, but it had something to do with the way they interacted with each other. She felt like they had feelings for each other beyond the normal love of a brother and sister. Still, she had fallen hard for Ray during their short time together, so she forced the thoughts of any oddity out of mind. She packed her suitcase for the trip to New York City.

Later than night, Janet followed the same routine as the previous evening. Believing Martha to be asleep, Janet went to Ray's bedside and stayed there for over two hours. They caressed and petted short of actual intercourse until nearly 3:00 a.m. as Martha listened in her bed just three feet away.

On Monday morning, Ray and Janet went to three banks, leaving Martha behind at the apartment. Ray's power of persuasion had worked again. He figured the more money Janet had on her, the more money he would be able to get. Janet had accounts at the three different banks at the insistence of her lawyer. He believed her money would be safer that way.

At Albany Savings Bank, Janet withdrew jewelry, bonds, and cash from her safe deposit box, and also closed her savings account, walking out with over $2000 in cash. At the Irving Bank & Trust Company, Ray watched as Janet withdrew the entire amount of her account, nearly $1900 total. She took $1500 of it via a cashier's check made out to herself, taking the remaining $400 as cash. At their next stop, Mechanics and Farmers Savings Bank, Janet again withdrew the entire amount of the account in the form of a $2000 check payable to The First National Bank of New York. Once Janet had emptied all of her accounts, Ray employed all of his powers of persuasion to get control over the funds.

"Darling, I must say that I'm a little concerned with you carrying around so much money," Ray told her, adopting an appropriately serious tone.

"You're right, I'll feel safer if you have it," Janet replied.

Without a second thought she handed over all of the checks and cash to her future husband, nearly $6000 in total (the equivalent of over $62,000 in 2019 adjusted for inflation).

"If it will make you feel better, I'll gladly hold onto them for you," he said, sharing a radiant smile as he put them in his jacket pocket. "I wouldn't want you to misplace them or, God forbid, have them stolen."

Despite Ray's warm demeanor, he was irritated that Janet had not withdrawn all of her savings in cash, but at least now he had control of the cashier checks. Having completed the bank errands, Ray and Janet returned to her Albany apartment to retrieve Janet's suitcase and pick up Martha. She greeted them warmly, as if she had not seen them in weeks, wearing a mask of happiness to conceal the jealousy smoldering deep within her eyes. The three then departed for Adeline Place, stopping on the way at Ray's sister's house at 1202 Astoria Drive in Astoria so he could pick up his mail. Rather than parking in the drive way, out front, or anywhere near his sister's home, Ray parked the car more than a block away. Leaving Martha and Janet in the car, he walked to the house and returned a few minutes later with the mail in hand. On the drive out of Albany, Ray spotted a New York Highway Patrol car parked near a bridge. Concerned about the snow and ice, he stopped to ask about the condition of the roads and the best route to take to New York City. After thanking the officer, Ray took the Northern State Parkway to Valley Stream.

It was nearly 9:00 p.m. when they arrived at Ray and Martha's Adeline Place apartment in Valley Stream. The three entered the apartment via the stairs in the front hallway of the house, out of sight of the separate entrance to the owner's ground floor residence located on the side of the building. Janet climbed the thirteen steps to the top of the stairway and entered Ray and Martha's apartment through the kitchen. While Martha gave her a quick tour of the small space, Ray went back to the car and took a hammer out of his tool box, a wood-handled Ballpein hammer with a flat end opposite the rounded knob instead of a two-pronged claw.

"What's that for?" Martha asked as he walked through the kitchen into the living room.

"I need to hang those pictures that fell down," he said, indicating a couple of frames propped against the wall on the floor. "Besides," he continued, careful not to let his voice carry, "we might need it later."

Martha gave him a concerned look. She could only guess at what he meant and in response she felt something between nervous dread and misplaced relief. While she busied herself with cooking dinner to take her mind off of it, Ray used the hammer to the hang the pictures, then tossed it on a living room chair.

During dinner, Janet discussed wedding plans with Ray, her excitement apparent from her rapid rate of speech. Afterward, they went back into the living room, while Martha washed dishes and cleaned up. While discussing how to tell her family and friends about their engagement, Ray suggested that he and Janet surprise them by sending sheets of paper with the word "Surprise!" at the top and Janet's signature at the bottom. They could then follow up the mysterious message a few days later with their official wedding announcement. Janet happily agreed to her Latin Lover's "cute" idea and they sat down at the dining room table so Janet could sign the "Surprise" papers. As she did so, Ray suggested that she endorse the two cashier's checks since she already had her fountain pen in hand. Worn down from the long day and eager to please her future husband, Janet blithely signed both the $1500 and $2000 checks before handing them back to Ray. Shortly after 10:00 p.m., Janet announced that she was tired and walked to the bathroom to take a warm bath before bed.

When Ray went into the kitchen a few minutes later, Martha remarked on what she had overheard.

"If I didn't see it, I wouldn't believe it," she said with amazement.

"What do you mean you wouldn't believe it?" Ray replied with a laugh.

"Right there and then you asked her to sign the checks and she was happy to do so."

Martha smiled her approval, admiring the resourcefulness of her handsome lover.

"That is what you get for being kind to a woman and giving her affection," he said with a wink.

Chapter Nine

The sleeping arrangement was similar to how it had been at Janet's apartment. Ray would sleep on the couch, while Martha and Janet shared a double bed in the only bedroom, surrounded by crucifixes and the votive candles Ray used for his Voodoo rituals. But Martha was not ready for bed yet. She wanted something before she could sleep.

While Janet enjoyed her bath, Martha came to Ray's bedside.

"I miss you baby," she said, rubbing her hands on his chest. "It's been three days since we've been together. I need you," she purred as her hands wandered down to his waist and kept rubbing. "I want you to go down on me."

"Martha, we can't," Ray sighed, pulling her hands away. "She could come out any time. We have to wait."

Martha stopped touching him and frowned.

"I guess you don't really love me," she mumbled before storming back into the bedroom.

Exasperated, Ray pulled his blanket back up and rolled over onto his side. Janet finished her bath around midnight and joined Martha in their shared bed. Despite the relaxing effects of her bath, Janet tossed and turned for a while, unable to sleep. She asked Martha about Ray's family, Martha's nursing career, and where Ray planned to live after he married Janet. The questions went on for quite some time before she finally fell asleep. Then she woke up again.

"Do you recall if Ray locked the front door?" she suddenly asked, apparently assuming that Martha shared her inability to sleep. She repeated the question, louder, when Martha failed to answer right away.

This time Martha heard her.

"I doubt it. We never lock it," Martha groaned, obviously annoyed at being disturbed just as she was falling asleep.

All was quiet for a few seconds as Janet considered her answer.

"We have quite a bit of money in the house to be sleeping with the door unlocked," she said nervously. "Anyone could come in and get it."

Janet's anxiety intensified as she stared into the darkness.

"In the morning, I'm taking all of the money to the bank myself to make sure it's safe," she said. "I want to make sure the checks are all safely deposited."

"Go to sleep," Martha told her, growing even more irritated and in a voice loud enough for Ray to hear her agitation in the living room. "It will be fine. We'll figure everything out in the morning."

But her assurance did nothing to calm Janet.

"Please don't patronize me, Martha," she shot back, sitting up in bed. "I think I ought to call my sister-in-law and ask her about what to do."

Now Martha sat up too.

"Don't be silly, Janet. Look at the hour. It's nearly 3:00 a.m. She's sound asleep. You can call her in the morning. Besides, the phone is downstairs and you'll wake the landlord if you go down there now. I'll go down in the morning and help you look her up in the phone book."

Martha could not take it any longer. She rolled out of bed and stomped into the living room where Ray was sleeping on the pull-out sofa bed.

"For God's sake, give her back her checks," Martha bellowed.

"Have her get dressed, take her to the train, and send her back to Albany!"

Ray sat up and stared blankly at her, still not quite awake.

Wearing her cotton nightgown, Janet followed Martha into the living room. She stood beside her brown leather suitcase that was on the floor next to the sofa bed.

"I don't want to leave," she yelled. "I want to stay, and I don't want the checks."

"Then what do you want?" Ray asked.

"I don't know what I want," Janet screamed. "I don't know. I have to think things out."

Ray glanced at Martha as Janet kneeled down and started pulling clothes out of her suitcase.

"We've got to get her quiet," he murmured under his breath.

But Janet saw Martha nod in response.

"Janet, go back to bed," Ray said, "we'll settle this all in the morning."

Janet glared at Martha.

"Are you telling him what to do?" she demanded.

"I'm not telling him anything," Martha replied. "The people downstairs are sleeping and we can sort this out in the morning. He's my brother and I don't want him to get into any trouble with the landlord."

Janet stopped looking through her suitcase and turned to face Martha. She was tired and anxious and ill-tempered. She was not in the mood to be told what to do, and she resented Martha for treating her like a child.

"I know he's your brother, but soon Charles will be my husband," she told Martha, her voice rising even more. "And I want you to know that as soon as we're married, you'll be leaving. You won't be living with us anymore."

"What?" Martha sneered. "Don't tell me you're jealous of his sister!"

"From what I've seen the past few days, I have every right to be!"

"Janet, why don't you let Martha give you some pills to calm you down and help you sleep," Ray suggested in a way that sounded more like a command. "We can sort all of this out in the morning," he added. "It will be easier to understand when you're rested."

But Janet was too worked-up to think of anything else. She touched Ray's arm and started sobbing.

"Is my money safe?" she whimpered.

"Of course, it is," Ray replied, growing angry from Janet's whimpering. "It's still in my pocket and I haven't gone out since you gave it to me."

He glared at Martha.

"What happened?" he asked. "Did you tell her something?"

"No," Martha replied indignantly. "I didn't tell her anything."

Still sobbing, Janet turned around and bent over her suitcase again, frantically sorting through her clothes.

"Get her quiet," Ray barked. "I don't care how." With that he stormed out of the room and closed the bathroom door behind him. After a few moments, Martha shouted his name. When he returned to the living room, he saw Janet sprawled on the floor with blood all over her head, and Martha was standing over her holding a hammer.

She had grabbed the hammer off the chair where Ray tossed it earlier that evening, and as Janet knelt over her suitcase, Martha had raised the hammer above her. Using all of her strength, she had swung it down onto the back of Janet's head with a dull thud. Janet had slumped sideways over her suitcase and began groaning loudly. Martha had quickly struck again, smashing the hammer against Janet's head with another sickening thump.

Now, as Janet continued to moan, Martha took a step back and dropped the bloody hammer onto the floor.

"Finish it," she told Ray, her eyes now empty and blank.

Ray stepped over to Janet and grabbed her throat with both hands. The mortally wounded woman groaned faintly as he strangled her, squeezing and straining to crush her windpipe.

"You can't do it that way," Martha told him. She grabbed a white, silk scarf that was draped on a nearby chair and tied the scarf around Janet's neck. The fabric quickly became saturated with the blood oozing from her head.

As Martha struggled to maintain her grip, Ray lifted the hammer from the floor and inserted its handle into the scarf. Seizing the handle firmly with both hands, he twisted it tight like a tourniquet, wrenching the scarf tightly around Janet's neck. He kept strangling her until he was sure she was dead, keeping a steady grip on the handle until Janet lay utterly quiet and still.

Releasing the tourniquet, Ray let Janet slump onto her back beside her suitcase. Blood was already pooling on the floor.

"My God, Darling," Martha gasped, "what have we done?"

Ray shuffled over to the bookcase where a bottle of Cream of Coca, a souvenir from Cuba, stood next to a bottle of Three Feathers whiskey and a couple of empty glasses. He poured a glassful of whiskey and gulped it down in one shot. Then he did the same with another.

"Do you think anyone heard anything?" he asked.

Martha joined him, drinking a couple of shots herself.

"No, but we've got to do something about the blood," she said, "or it will seep through the floor."

If their landlords, the Arnsperger family, living on the first floor below saw the blood, they would be as good as caught. Martha hastened to the bathroom and retrieved some cloth along with a white wash basin with some water in it. Using an old magazine, she scooped up the pooling blood and poured it into the basin. Then the two of them used the cloth to soak up the rest of the blood from the floor before it could seep down into the stucco. Mopping briskly with Clorox took care of the blood that had already hardened. As Martha finished with the floor, Ray took the bloody hammer into the kitchen and washed it in the sink.

Now they needed to dispose of the body. Martha slipped two rings off of Janet's fingers to pawn them later, and retrieved the lower plate of Janet's dentures from the floor where it had fallen while Ray strangled her. She also removed the top plate from Janet's mouth. Martha knew that getting rid of them would make identification of her body more difficult if it was discovered. They put a white Turkish towel over Janet's face, wrapped a pale-blue drape around her body, and tied her up with clothesline that they kept in the bathroom. Then they bent her legs and tied them in a jackknife position with her knees pressed up against her chest. Martha took off the red chenille robe she had been wearing and tossed it onto Janet's body too. The robe was too blood-stained to keep.

Having bound her body, they dragged the corpse into the closet, a temporary hiding place until they could come up with a permanent spot. They put a small trunk on the floor in front of the body to block anyone from seeing it if they happened to open the closet door. A thousand frantic thoughts flashed through their minds about how to get rid of the body.

"I'll have to wait until nightfall and then I can take the body to a bridge we've been working at and try to bury it there under the railway," Ray said at last.

"You can't do that, Honey," Martha replied, "there will be so many cars and trucks going by that you'll be spotted. You won't have a chance."

Ray realized she was right.

"The only way we can get it out of here without anyone seeing it is by putting it in the trunk," he said.

They went back to the closet and took the trunk out, then lifted the body out and lowered it into the trunk. It wouldn't fit. The trunk was too small. They had no choice but to return the body to the closet and put the trunk back in front of it. Frustrated, they racked their brains trying to figure out what to do. Finally, a suitable plan materialized. Now they just had to carry it out without being caught.

Chapter Ten

Having finished cleaning up the murder site, the two killers drove to Harlem later that morning. They purchased a large storage trunk at a luggage shop on 125th Street near Lenox Avenue and then went to the Jamaica area of Long Island in nearby Queens County. While Ray waited outside in the car, Martha walked into the Jamaica National Bank with the two cashier's checks that Janet Fay had endorsed shortly before her death. Martha tried opening a new checking account using the two checks and five $100 bills as an initial deposit, but the teller refused to accept the $2000 check payable to the First National Bank of New York and suggested that Martha take it there to cash. Frustrated, but with no other choice, she left without opening an account or cashing either of the cashier's checks.

From there, Ray and Martha headed to the familiar surroundings of New York City. On Wall Street, Martha entered the First National Bank. She explained to the bank clerk that the $2000 check payable to First National Bank had been given to her by Janet Fay in exchange for the sale of a trailer. Despite the seeming sincerity of Martha's story, the clerk declined to cash or deposit the check since Janet did not have an account at the bank. The clerk advised Martha to resolve the matter at

Mechanics and Farmers Savings Bank, the institution that issued the check.

So far unsuccessful in cashing the checks, Ray and Martha drove back to their Adeline Place apartment with the storage trunk to show for their efforts. They lugged the trunk upstairs, dragged Janet's body out of the closet, and dropped her into the trunk. They packed Martha's bloodied chenille robe around the body along with all of the clothes from Janet's suitcase and a pillow "to keep the body from shaking" and rustling around when they moved the trunk. After closing the top securely, they pushed the trunk up against the left side of the living room wall. They spread a tablecloth over the trunk, put a clock on top of it, and arranged their radio and record player in front of it.

Now the pair had a temporary hiding place for the body, but they still needed to find a permanent spot to get rid of it. They tossed around some possibilities, including throwing the body in a river "trunk and all," but worried that after sinking to the bottom it would come back the surface and float. They decided not to take the chance. Burying the body somewhere seemed the only good solution. Leaving the body at the apartment, they drove "all over the surrounding country" trying to scout for a suitable burial spot, but nothing fit their needs.

The next day, January 5, they drove to Janet's apartment in Albany and packed up all of her belongings. Then Martha visited Janet's landlord, Helen Bernard. Bearing an earnest expression, Martha informed her that because Janet would be marrying "Charles Martin" and moving in with him, she no longer needed her apartment. Since Janet was tired of driving back and forth between her new home and the Albany apartment, she had asked Martha to pack up her things and return the keys to Helen. As Martha handed over the keys, she assured Helen that Janet would write her a letter confirming everything.

Having taken care of Janet's apartment, Martha and Ray made their way to the Mechanics & Farmers Savings Bank in Albany. During the drive to the bank, Ray tossed Janet's denture plates out of the window to dispose of them, while Martha rehearsed what she would say to the bank officials. At the bank, she told the teller that the $2000 cashier's check had been given to her by a "man and lady as partial payment for a trailer they were buying to take a honeymoon in Florida." In what was by then becoming a slapstick loop of banking logic, the clerk refused to accept the check, telling her that she needed to cash it at First National Bank since that was the designated payee.

So far stymied in their efforts to abscond with Janet Fay's funds, the frustrated pair turned their attention to procuring an acceptable site for disposing of her corpse. They began house hunting in Westport, Connecticut, looking for a home that had a yard or garage or cellar, someplace private they could bury Janet's body without being seen. A couple prospects that sounded promising at first did not meet their needs for one reason or another after inspecting the sites in person.

On Friday, January 7, they drove back to the First National Bank on Wall Street where, after some calls to the Mechanic's and Farmer's Savings Bank, Martha was able to cash the $2000 check. From there, she opened a new account at the Long Island Savings Bank in Astoria by depositing the $1500 cashier's check payable to and endorsed by Janet Fay, along with $2500 cash. Having completed one task, they returned to another pressing matter. Janet's body still sat hidden in the storage trunk some three days after her murder and it was causing a noticeable stench in their Adeline Place apartment.

The following day, Ray and Martha carried the trunk down the stairway of their apartment and loaded it into the car. Then they drove to Ray's sister's house in Astoria and put the trunk in her cellar, another temporary hiding place until they secured a permanent disposal site. An unexpected obstacle arose when, out of concern that the trunk would mildew in the damp cellar, Ray's sister began insisting that they put it upstairs in the living room. Luckily, Ray's assurance that nothing in the trunk would be harmed by a little humidity finally convinced her to let them leave the trunk in the cellar. While they were there, Ray threw out a rug stained with Janet's blood by leaving it for the garbagemen to take along with his sister's garbage outside the house. They got rid of a bloody pillow that Martha had put under Janet's head by throwing it in the East River under the Triboro Bridge.

The next business day, Monday, January 10, they tried another branch of First National Bank, where Martha tendered the $2000 cashier's check payable to the bank and was ultimately able to collect the entire amount in cash. With all of Janet's funds now in hand, their final task focused on covering their tracks. Ray drove over to Bridge-port, Connecticut, where he had lived as a boy, hoping to find a house or yard that would be suitable for burying Janet's body. But he had no luck finding a place. Having learned during her late-night talks with Janet that Janet's step-daughter, Mary Spencer, was her closest family member, Martha suggested that they take steps to deflect suspicion of Janet's sudden disappearance and convince those who knew her that "she was still alive and happy and getting along all right." At Western Union, Martha sent a short telegram to Mary: *HAVING WONDERFUL TIME. EVERYTHING FINE. LETTER FOLLOWS. LOVE TO ALL. JANET.* Martha figured that would buy them some much needed time.

While Martha took care of one part of the scam, Ray found a house that fit their needs at 133-15 149th Street, South Ozone Park in Queens. The small, two-story building had an easily accessible basement that would allow them to complete their grisly task without being seen. They retrieved the trunk from the cellar of Ray's sister's home and borrowed a pick and shovel from her. That night, he broke into a construction company warehouse where he had once worked, stealing several bags of cement to complete the necessary preparations.

Over the following day and night, Ray used the borrowed pick to break through the concrete floor of the Ozone Park rental house base-ment and then dug Janet Fay's grave: a six-foot deep hole next to the cellar's oil-burning furnace. When the hole was ready, Martha helped him lift Janet's body out of the trunk and lower it into the newly exposed earth. They covered the body before filling the hole back in with the displaced soil, careful not to leave any piles of dirt that might attract attention. To finish up the concealment process, Ray covered the grave by spreading the stolen cement across it, smoothing the cement out and setting up a fan to help it dry. Confident no one would ever be able to find Janet's body, the two had sex to celebrate successful completion of the job.

Later, noticing an odor and large blood stain in the trunk that had held Janet's body, Ray painted over it with some varnish he found in the cellar of the rental home. When the odor persisted, Ray and Martha took the trunk back to their Adeline Place apartment, where they put wallpaper over the entire inside of the trunk to obscure the smell.

When the cement concealing Janet's grave completely hardened three days later, Ray informed their rental agent that the house did not suit them after all, and they would no longer be staying there. Though surprised by their quick change of mind, the agent raised no protest since they did not request a refund of any of the first month's rent they had paid. From there, they visited a car dealership in Long Island City, and traded-in their 1946 Pontiac toward a 1948 model for the trade value plus $1200 cash. Then Ray went back to work at T. & T. Construction.

A couple of days later on January 17, the first Volkswagen Beetle arrived in New York City from Germany. The "people's car" or "Volkswagen" had been designed and constructed at the behest of the Nazi leader, Adolf Hitler, who wanted a cheap car mass-produced for the German people. Though originally a dud in the United States with only two cars sold in 1949 during the entire year, the Beetle would go on to become a huge success.

To alleviate suspicion and give them more time to distance themselves from the crime, Ray prepared the letter from "Janet Fay" that had been promised in the telegram Martha sent to Mary Spencer a few days earlier. Using one of the blank papers previously signed by Janet, he erased the word "Surprise" at the top by using Clorox, and then typed the fake letter:

Dear Mary,

I am all excited and having the time of my life. I never felt as happy before. I soon will be Mrs. Martin and will go to Florida.

Mary, I am about to ask you a great favor. I would like you to call on the American Express Agency and have them ship my trunks and boxes that I have there to me. The address is on the various stickers that I am enclosing in the letter.

I would like to sort out many things before I leave for Florida. I am so happy and contented, for Charles is so good and nice to me and also his family. They have done everything to make me feel comfortable and at home.

I will close now with my best wishes for you both and love and kisses for the children. I really do miss you all but I am sure that my prayers are granted to me by sending me this wonderful man.

God bless you all,

Janet J. Fay

Pleased by his handiwork, Ray sealed the letter in an envelope and dropped it in the next public mailbox he came across. However, what he did not realize was that a fundamental fact would doom the ruse to failure: namely that Janet Fay had never owned a typewriter. Indeed, Janet did not even know how to type. Mary Spencer knew that Janet could not type so when she received the letter, she quickly became suspicious. With a few inquiries, she found out that Janet's home had been sold for $6,000 and that all of the funds in her account at an Albany bank had been withdrawn. Her suspicion now increased to full-fledged concern about Janet's well-being, Mary took the letter to the police and reported her stepmother as a missing person.

Chapter Eleven

C onfident that they had successfully covered their tracks, Ray and Martha made their way to Chicago, arriving on January 18. They discussed the possibility of continuing west and moving to Alaska, but decided Chicago would be a good place to lay low for a while. In the meantime, they needed more money to pay for the potential cross-country relocation and support the start of a new life together. Lacking another source for an inflow of funds, Ray returned to the lonely hearts well.

Reading through the latest batch of letters from his ardent correspondents, he chose Deliphene Downing, a 41-year-old widow from Wyoming Township, Michigan, a suburb about ten miles south of Grand Rapids in Kent County, Michigan. Deliphene's letter had arrived at Ray's sister's house on January 4, the very date of Janet Fay's murder. Ray no doubt found the timing amusing. He certainly noticed Deliphene's loneliness and readily concluded that she would be an easy conquest unable to resist his Voodoo spells and seductive charm.

He was right about Deliphene feeling lonely. Her husband, Rolland, an Air Force veteran who fought in World War II, had died two years earlier in a devastating accident. His truck was struck in Grand Rapids by a Pennsylvania railroad train travelling 60 miles per hour. The train struck the driver's side of Rolland's truck with such force that the truck was demolished and Rolland was thrown 90 feet through the air. In a cruel twist of fate, the company that employed Rolland owned the very train that killed him. Rolland and Deliphene's daughter, Rainelle, was five months old at the time.

In Deliphene's letters to him, Ray picked up right away that Rainelle, now two-years-old, had become the focus of Deliphene's life. Ray crafted his letters to Deliphene accordingly, sometimes having Martha help him to express how much "Charles Martin" adored children, a shrewd artifice that maximized his appeal in the love-lorn widow's eyes. In a revealing letter to Ray, Deliphene had written:

> *Dear Charles,*
>
> *Thank you for your thoughtful Christmas greetings. Christmas is so busy with its hustle and bustle and the lull afterwards is such a letdown. It gives me an empty, lonely feeling.*
>
> *New Year's Eve I kept the neighbor's children so they could go out and the children were sleeping peacefully when the whistles blew. The only noise was when a dog sat up howling at midnight.*
>
> *....*
>
> *Rainelle got a tricycle from some friends and she is sitting on it now and really making a noise. Do you like children's carols? I hope you do, for if we continue to correspond, I will mention Rainelle often.*
>
> *I hope I don't break the rules of our friendship correspondence by writing you before I give you time to consider my last letter.*
>
> *Sincerely,*
>
> *Deliphene*

Ray's technique of written romance worked just as it had with his prior amorous pen pals. Like clockwork, after exchanging several ardent letters with Deliphene, she invited Ray to meet her in person. On January 22, he brought Martha with him to Deliphene's home at 3435 Byron Center Road in Wyoming Township and introduced her yet again as his sister. After meeting "Charles" in person, Deliphene instantly fell under the spell of his courtesy and charm. She also enjoyed the company of Martha, who she found "jolly" and "loads of fun." From his perspective, Ray was pleasantly surprised to find that Deliphene was prettier than he had imagined. She had a whole-some looking attractiveness, a girl-next-door, beguiling beauty that made it feel more natural – less deceitful – when they became sexually inti-mate. Before long, they began planning a New York marriage. But Ray's eyes remained fixed firmly on the real prize. All the while, he schemed how to convert Deliphene's assets into cash.

Enamored with her new Romeo, Deliphene took him to meet her parents in Palisade, Nebraska. Always the schmoozer, Charles Martin's charm readily won her family's approval. Indeed, Deliphene's sister voiced the unanimous view that he seemed a "very pleasant" fellow.

Deliphene could not believe her good fortune. After suffering the tragic loss of her husband, she feared that she would have to raise Rainelle as a single mom. Although not unheard of at the time, it was certainly unusual and just as certain to involve hardship, not the least of which would be a constant underlying loneliness. Yet, against all odds, she had found a kind man, a good man who loved her and adored her daughter. Deliphene could not stop talking about him to her friends, who were genuinely happy for her despite noticing how much less she visited them after this new suitor came to Wyoming Township and entered her life.

By February 26, after more than two weeks of enjoying Charles's affections, Deliphene became concerned about missing her normal menstrual cycle. Fearful that a pregnancy before marriage might scare Charles away, Deliphene sought help from Martha, who she had come to trust like a real sister.

Martha saw her chance to be rid of the latest rival for Ray's atten-tion. Concealing the possessive jealousy that once again threatened to erupt, Martha assumed the role of sympathetic confidant.

"I know just the thing to take care of it," she assured Deliphene with secret glee.

As Rainelle played quietly in her mother's room, Martha gave Deliphene a handful of pills and a glass of water, promising that taking the pills would abort the pregnancy. Deliphene graciously availed herself of her future sister-in-law's help. Soon after swallowing the pills, Deliphene felt ill. She went into the bathroom feeling nauseas, but came back out a short time later after noticing blood in her underwear.

"Good news," she said with a faint smile. "It was a false alarm. I'm not pregnant after all. But I do feel really drowsy."

Deliphene stumbled clumsily across the room and collapsed onto her bed. Seeing her mother in such a condition frightened Rainelle and she started crying with a loud wail. Her nerves already on edge from watching Ray cohort with yet another woman, something snapped in Martha. She grabbed Rainelle by the throat and squeezed, choking her until the crying stopped and her face began turning blue.

Having heard the commotion, Ray hurried into the room and saw Martha with her hands around the little girl's neck.

"For God's sake, Martha, what are you doing?" he exclaimed.

Martha stared back at him blankly. Then they heard a noise. As if roused by her daughter's distress, Deliphene began to stir, trying to shake off the effect of the sleeping pills that Martha had given her. She struggled to lift her head and sit up.

"If she wakes up she'll go to the police," Martha hissed, fearing that Deliphene would see the bruise marks on Rainelle's neck. "Do something!"

Ray rushed into the adjacent room and grabbed a service revolver that had belonged to Deliphene's deceased husband. Spying a pink baby blanket in Rainelle's crib, he wrapped it around the pistol as a temporary silencer. Darting back into the bedroom, he moved next to the bed and motioned for Martha to take Rainelle into another room. He pointed the gun at Deliphene's head and pulled the trigger. Then he fired a second bullet into her brain to finish the job. The shots roared loudly in the small confines of the room and Ray's ears hummed despite using the make-shift silencer.

In the silence that followed, Martha returned from the other room with some bed sheets and helped him swaddle Deliphene's body. After wrapping her, they carried Deliphene down to the cellar. Following the same method that they used to bury Janet Fay, Ray used a pick to break through the cement floor, then dug a hole in the exposed earth. After a few feet of digging, water began accumulating in the bottom of the pit. The pooling water increased as Ray dug deeper and they had to use buckets to bail the water into two nearby washtubs.

When they were satisfied that it was deep enough, Ray and Martha dumped Deliphene's corpse into the hole. Just as he had done before, Ray filled the hole with the displaced dirt and covered the grave with newly poured cement.

The deed done, they collapsed onto Deliphene's bed.

"What do we do now?" Ray asked, the weak tone of his voice echoing his exhaustion.

Martha hesitated. She waited for a sign of the suave, self-confident man that had mesmerized her from the start.

"I'll go to the police and tell them I did it," she said finally. "By the time they suspect anything else, you'll be long gone. At least one of us could make it to Alaska that way."

Ray shook his head, refusing to even entertain the idea.

"No, we're staying together, darling," he told her, once again playing the role of chivalrous lover. "No matter what."

Hoping to alleviate suspicion about Deliphene's absence, they paid a visit to her neighbors, telling them that she had left on an emergency trip to visit a sick relative, but had asked the two of them to stay at the house and take care of Rainelle. The neighbors reacted with surprise, but seemed to accept Ray's explanation. After thinking through their options, Ray and Martha decided the best course of action would be to take Rainelle with them back to New York. However, an unforeseen problem arose: the child drew away from them in fear whenever they came close to her. If they were going to risk taking her to New York, they needed to find a way to gain her trust first.

Chapter Twelve

Over the next two days, Ray and Martha tried to gain Rainelle's trust, but nothing worked. Even buying her a puppy at a nearby farmhouse failed to win her over. The child remained wary of them, as if sensing that they had done something terrible to her mother. Eventually, Ray decided they could not afford to keep Rainelle alive. It would be too hard maintaining a believable story as to why she was with them, particularly since she cried all of the time and refused to eat.

"We're already in this thing deep," Ray told Martha. "We're going to have to get rid of her."

"How?" she replied.

"That's up to you. You can leave her somewhere as far as I'm concerned. I don't care what you do, just get rid of her."

"We can't leave her at a shelter," Martha protested. "They'll be too many questions."

"Then smother her with a pillow, anything, just get rid of her before her crying brings the whole neighborhood over here."

Martha hesitated. Rainelle reminded her of her own daughter.

"I can't do it, Ray," she said tearing up. "I just can't."

But something in his eyes convinced her she could. The thought of displeasing him overcame anything else. Steadying her nerves, she bent over and lifted Rainelle off the floor. Martha carried her down to the basement beside the two washtubs still filled with the brackish water bailed from Deliphene's grave. Martha quietly undressed the little girl, gingerly as if getting ready to give her a bath before bedtime. She looked into Rainelle's eyes and smiled. Suddenly, she grabbed Rainelle's legs and yanked her into the air. Gripping her tightly by the feet, Martha flipped her upside down and dunked the terrified girl headfirst into the tub. Rainelle kicked and thrashed for her life, twisting violently and churning the muddy tub water into a frothy storm as she clawed at Martha's arms. After what seemed an eternity, the little girl's struggling slowed, and then she was still. Martha held her limp body in the dark water for another ten or fifteen minutes. She wanted to be sure. She waited a while longer and then slowly let go, staggering away from the tub in a trance before numbly shuffling back up the cellar stairs.

Ray buried Rainelle next to her mother in another hole in the cellar, spreading a fresh layer of concrete over the grave to conceal it under the basement floor. He had barely finished when someone knocked on the front door. It was Deliphene's neighbors. They wanted to check on Rainelle and make sure everything was okay. Ray smiled broadly, spinning a convincing yarn about having taken Rainelle to Deliphene's mother-in-law. Apparently satisfied with the explanation, the neighbors thanked him and left, but in truth they remained suspicious. They knew how protective Deliphene was when it came to Rainelle. They found it hard to believe that she would ever leave Rainelle in the care of someone she had only recently met.

Having disposed of the evidence of yet another murder, Ray and Martha could have fled to Alaska as they previously discussed, or anywhere else for that matter. Instead, they did something peculiar. Rather than taking what they had fleeced from Deliphene and leaving the area, they drove into town to see a movie. When they returned to Deliphene's house a few hours later, they hardly hung their coats in the closet when someone knocked at the door. It was just after 11:00 p.m.

Ray opened the door to find two men standing outside.

"Good evening, sir. Could you please tell me your name?" one asked.

"Charles Martin. And may I ask who you are?" Ray replied.

"I'm Detective Vander Band of the Kent County Sheriff's Office. Are you not Raymond Fernandez?"

Ray's courteous smile wavered into a startled expression, but only for a moment.

"If you already know that's my name, then it must be so," Ray responded, resuming his pleasant manner.

"We'd like to talk to you about the disappearance of Deliphene Downing," the detective continued.

Ray glanced at Martha and flashed her a reassuring smile.

"Disappearance? I think there's been some confusion, officer."

"What do you mean?" Vander Band asked.

"Well, I know Deliphene went to Detroit to visit some friends," Ray replied. "We're just watching the place for her until she returns."

"What about her little girl, Rainelle?" the detective pressed.

"She went with her mom to Detroit," Ray said without batting an eye.

"Well, Ms. Downing's neighbors are quite concerned about her. Do you mind if we take a look around the house?"

"Not at all, officers. Go right ahead," Ray replied, smugly confident in his handiwork in concealing the bodies.

Deliphene's neighbors, suspicious that she and Rainelle had disappeared without telling anyone that they planned on travelling anywhere, had called the police requesting they do a welfare check on her as well as looking into the couple who had moved into Deliphene's home.

"We don't mean to be a nosey neighborhood – just neighborly," said neighbor Newell Burt. She told police that it had been the "talk of the block" how "Charles" had suddenly moved in with Deliphene and monopolized her time, taking her away from her long-time friends.

"I didn't like him," Burt explained. "He was supposed to be a wealthy man from New York, but he didn't look and act the part."

Her suspicion grew exponentially when she saw him driving a new car the day after Deliphene sold her five-room cottage.

"We put two and two together and decided they were milking Della of her money," she said sadly.

While detectives continued questioning Ray and Martha, police searching Deliphene's house discovered the two freshly cemented areas in the cellar. It did not take them long to break through the cement and dig down to the bodies. Indeed, Rainelle's body was still warm when police unearthed it, and the coroner called to the scene concluded the little girl had been dead for only a few hours.

Ray and Martha were immediately arrested. In addition to Ray having $4000 in cash, police found a list of more than 100 names of women from 12 states on a lonely hearts circular, 17 with check marks by their names and notations about money or property owned, who Ray referred to as "likely prospects":

> Janet J. Fay, 40, Albany, New York, $6000.
> Myra Alderman, Mendenhall, Mississippi, $8000.
> Hazel Hardy, Yermo, California, "owns property".
> Ruby Davis, High Point, North Carolina.
> Marian Cook, Grand Rapids, Michigan.
> Edith Johnson, Wakefield, Nebraska, "owns home and has $7000".
> Agnes Denyer, Detroit, Michigan, "owns home and has $10,000".
> Nella Stone, Mansfield, Pennsylvania, "savings and car".
> Jane Mason, Columbus, Ohio, $5500.
> Marva Olson, Tacoma, Washington, "home and savings".
> Annie Selansky, Dorchester, Massachusetts, $5000.
> Alice Jackson, Fremont, Nebraska, "home and savings".

Anna Meyers, Niles, Michigan, $5000.
Martha Scrodham, Mishawaka, Indiana.
Mrs. Thomas Green, Coldbrook, New York, $1000.
Prudie Gardner, Hooks, Texas, $3500.
Ollie Mitchell, Hays, North Carolina, "owns home."
Grace Vanluven, Detroit, Michigan, $4000.

Searchers also found a .22 caliber rifle and four boxes of .22 caliber long cartridges. A subsequent search of the trunk of Ray and Martha's car turned up a blood-stained Ballpein hammer.

Detectives took Ray and Martha downtown to the Wyoming Township Police Station where they were questioned until 3:00 in the morning, then transported to the Kent County Jail in Grand Rapids where they were photographed and fingerprinted. Eerily evocative of the Voodoo powers he claimed to possess, Ray left a lasting impression on his interrogators. They were "particularly struck by his eyes. They were brown, but there was something in them that is hard to explain. It was a smoldering quality – not fury, colder than that – and they were a trifle blank."

Not long after being fingerprinted, Ray and Martha were taken before a judge for their initial appearance. The press was waiting. Two or three photographers stood on each side of the judge taking pictures, their flash bulbs blinding the bewildered pair as the judge read the charges against them.

"There was so much noise in the courtroom," Martha recalled, "there was so much mumbling, the flash bulbs were [going off] – I had never been in any trouble before; I had never been in a courtroom; I didn't know what it was all about."

Following their brief court appearance, Ray and Martha were separated onto different floors of the jail. Martha had a cell on the third floor, while Ray was kept on the second level of the facility. They were interrogated by a new batch of investigators until Grand Rapids District Attorney, Roger McMahon, arrived at the jail. He spoke with Martha alone first, trying to persuade her to admit her involvement in Janet Fay's disappearance, promising a "much lighter" sentence in the

Downing murder case in exchange for her cooperation with New York investigators. However, Martha refused to discuss anything specific about the New York case without first talking to Ray. Her only comment about the case was that after Janet Fay spent the night at the Valley Stream apartment, she had left the next morning and Martha had not seen her since.

Shortly after 9:30 a.m., guards led Ray into a small room where McMahon and Martha awaited along with Kent County Deputy Sheriff Clarence Randle, a grey-haired veteran lawman with a square face and thick chin. Deputy Sheriff James Toohey and FBI Special Agent Robert Lalley were also in the room, along with Detective John Vander Band, a cocky personality who Martha quickly came to dislike because "he thought he was God's gift to detectives." There were other investigators in the room as well, including detectives from Chicago, Los Angeles, Wyoming, and elsewhere who wanted to know if Ray and Martha were connected to crimes committed in their jurisdictions.

"Time for you to come clean," McMahon told Ray. "You're in a bad jam for sure, but the truth is always the best way out of a bad jam. So how about it – what happened to Janet Fay?"

Ray smirked a little, but remained silent, his eyes shifting from McMahon to Martha and back to McMahon. Not dissuaded, the district attorney continued fishing for information.

"I can tell you that if you committed any crimes in states other than Michigan, if you're found guilty of the Michigan crimes and serve time for them, then you won't be prosecuted for any crimes committed in another state, whether it is South, North, East, or West," McMahon asserted.

Ray studied McMahon's face.

"How do I know that what you're telling me is true?" Ray asked after some moments of silence.

Now it was McMahon's turn to study the features of the man sitting across from him. But Ray's face was a stone wall and his eyes offered no window to his soul.

"I give you my solemn promise as the District Attorney of Kent County that what I've said is true," McMahon assured him.

Ray chuckled to himself and nodded.

"Why are you so concerned about what happened in other states when you work for Michigan?"

"I just want a statement for my own personal use," McMahon explained. "But I assure you that will be the extent of it. It won't be used against you."

Ray locked eyes with McMahon as if trying to read his mind, then smiled and looked over at Martha.

"You might as well go ahead and tell him about the other three," he sighed.

Before Martha could say anything, McMahon led her to another interview room, leaving Ray with the other investigators.

"Tell me about Janet Fay," McMahon prodded. "You didn't mention Janet before, but I think you should this time."

Having received Ray's okay, Martha gave a statement implicating them in Janet Fay's murder, as well as that of Deliphene and Rainelle Downing. When she was done, McMahon went back to the room where he had left Ray.

"Martha told me everything," he said. "We know what happened, but now I want to hear it from you. Make a clean slate of everything and tell the truth. The *whole* truth," he emphasized.

Ray leaned back in his chair.

"I'm not an ordinary criminal," he said with a sly smile, "but you got me dead to rights."

Chapter Thirteen

The interrogation continued from the early morning hours of March 1 well into the afternoon. Ray answered questions about Janet Fay's murder and discussed the Deliphene and Rainelle Downing killings like someone indignantly blaming traffic for why they were late for work. He admitted his involvement in Janet's murder, but insisted that it was not a premeditated act.

"It was when our plans went haywire that we resorted to murder," he said, maintaining that he had not planned on killing anyone ahead of time. He had merely reacted to the situation he found himself in. "What else could I do?" he asserted. "Once I was in, there I was."

Upon confirming Ray and Martha's involvement in Janet Fay's murder, the Michigan investigators alerted their New York counterparts. After initial conversations with the Grand Rapids Police Department, police in Nassau County, New York spent nearly a day digging up the basement of the Ozone Park rental home in Queens with nothing to show for it. As a crowd of curious neighbors gathered outside the home, two members of New York City Police Emergency Squad 17 used short-handled shovels to dig for what Ray and Martha had buried in the basement. Following more detailed directions given over the phone by Ray to the Queens County District Attorney, they unearthed a tiny piece of cloth bearing the name of James A. Paul, an Albany optometrist, buried three feet underground. Digging deeper, they unearthed Janet's corpse six feet under the cellar floor. In the dark of the night, three uniformed policemen, wearing heavy coats to ward off the cold, carried Janet's bagged body up the stairs, lifting it through the outside opening of the cellar doors into the still-white snow.

Around 10:00 that night, Deputy Sheriff Arnold Pigorsh came to Martha's cell door and asked for her address when she lived in Chicago. After she told him the South Washtenau Avenue address, he remarked, "Well, you have got enough to worry over. Did you know that Myrtle Young was dead?" With that, he turned around and walked away, leaving Martha to spend a worried, sleepless night in her cell.

The next day, Dr. Jacob Werne, Assistant Medical Examiner for Nassau County, conducted an autopsy of the "badly decomposed" body of Janet Fay. He found the body *trussed up with twine into the position of a jack-knife...the head bent on the trunk, the arms folded and brought close to the trunk, the lower extremities folded onto the trunk, and the lower extremities themselves flexed at the knees against the chest.*

Two circular wounds on Janet's head passed through skin and bone, entering her cranial cavity. One wound was located high on the back of Janet's head and the other was visible above her right ear. She also suffered a fractured larynx. In Dr. Werne's opinion, while either of the two wounds would have eventually caused Janet's death, the fracture of her larynx occurred before she died and would have caused her death in and of itself within two or three minutes. Dr. Theodore Curphey, Chief Medical Examiner of Nassau County, also examined Janet's body. Like Werne, he concluded that Janet died by strangulation, although either of the skull fractures would have eventually killed her as well. Their findings contradicted Inspector Stu Pinnell who had asserted to newspaper reporters: "It's 99-to-1 that the cause of death will be found to be fracture of the skull caused by blows from behind by a heavy instrument."

As news of the duo's arrest came out, reactions were mixed. Martha's brother, Dudley Seabrook, a Pensacola policeman, told reporters: "I just can't understand it."

Sheriff Marshall Hayes of Milton, Florida, proclaimed: "There wasn't a nicer girl in town than Martha."

A former teacher of Martha's shared: "I'm not only surprised. I'm greatly shocked."

Similarly, Ray and Martha's landlady for the Washtenaw Avenue apartment they had rented in Chicago remembered them as a "very nice couple – so quiet, so genteel."

While no one could believe Martha capable of murder, the same could not be said about Ray. When contacted by investigators about Ray's arrest, Esther Henne detailed how he had swindled her. Although he had been sweet at first, his true nature ultimately surfaced.

"I'll never forget it," she said. "It was a month of nightmares. The tongue lashings and verbal beatings he gave me were out of this world."

She eventually became suspicious about Ray and Martha's behavior toward one another.

"They acted too lovingly to be relatives," Esther explained.

The fallout from her relationship with Ray continued ever after she escaped his immediate influence. Forced to take an indefinite leave of absence from her job as a teacher at Pennhurst State school due to the mob of reporters staked out at her dormitory, Esther issued a statement to the International News Service:

When I first heard about the murders to which Raymond Fernandez is said to have confessed, I was very shocked but not surprised.

Throughout our marriage I was afraid of him. He continually carried on like a raving maniac and kept yelling and screaming at me.

We were married on February 28, 1948, and he was then a very charming man.

On March 8, $500 cash, my wedding ring, diamond ring, and wristwatch were taken [by Martha] from my New York apartment.

Twice I suspected them of giving me sleeping pills. It was then that the seed of suspicion entered my mind.

Esther felt certain that if she had not given thousands of dollars and a car to Ray and Martha, she would have shared the fate of Janet Fay and Deliphene Downing. Her suspicion reinforced investigators' belief that the duo, now dubbed the "Lonely Hearts Killers," had been slipping their victims phenobarbital or some form of derivative of it.

That belief gained further support when Catherine Tostrud came forward in St. Paul, Minnesota identifying Ray and Martha as the duo who fleeced her out of $4,000 in May 1948, then knocked her out for several days with an overdose of sleeping pills. Detectives became convinced that countless other women who had been victimized by Ray were too embarrassed to report it. And the FBI disclosed that it had been searching for Ray as the chief suspect in the case of a man who had been traveling around the country representing himself to wealthy widows as a "well-to-do former Secret Service man."

Informed of Ray and Martha's arrests and confessions, Pearl Wilson, mother of Jane Thompson, dolefully recalled Jane's trip to Spain with Ray. She did not beat around the bush about what happened to Jane.

"I'm sure now that my daughter was murdered," she said.

Chapter Fourteen

O n the heels of the murders of Deliphene and Rainelle Downing, the tone of the Michigan legislature, which had been weighing for some time whether to adopt capital punishment in the state, turned toward a more serious consideration of that possibility. Debate on a bill in the House of Representatives had been under way for over an hour when Louis Crampton, a former circuit court judge and the Republican representative from Lapeer, read aloud from a newspaper article about the Downing double murder. The politician's voice quivered as he proclaimed the necessity for "the punishment to fit the crime." Also arguing in favor of the bill was Representative Andrew Bolt, the Republican congressman from Grand Rapids, who proclaimed that the Downing killings proved that "all murders are not committed by mentally deficient persons as many believe." Despite the surge of support for capital punishment, those opposing the death penalty also rallied together, bound by their concern that an innocent man might mistakenly be put to death.

"If the sponsors can assure me that human judgment is infallible, I will vote for the bill," bellowed Representative Ed Carey of Detroit.

Opponents proposed amendments designed to "laugh down" the bill, such as proposals to make the sponsors of the bill the "executioners," and those calling for the infliction of the death penalty by "stoning to death as the gates of the city" or "asphyxiation by drowning," a particularly disturbing proposal given Rainelle Downing's manner of death.

As the debate continued among the politicians, Deliphene's father arrived from Nebraska to claim his daughter's and his grand-daughter's bodies, and to arrange for their transport back to Palisade for burial in the family's church plot.

In early March 1949, the Michigan Legislature rejected the bill calling for automatic imposition of the death penalty for first degree murder by a vote of 51 to 44. However, another bill granting the trial judge the discretion to impose a death sentence passed 53 to 10.

While passing each other briefly in the jail, Ray and Martha saw each other for the first time since being taken into custody. They exchanged rueful smiles and some quick words.

"Will you write to me, honey?" Ray asked. "I still love you."

"Where we're going, we'll be too far apart to write," Martha replied.

"We'll probably wind up in Hell," Ray added with a cavalier laugh.

"Yeah, in a front seat," Martha agreed jokingly.

While investigators reviewed lists of missing women in a dozen states to determine whether they crossed paths with Ray and Martha, Roger McMahon disclosed to reporters that prosecutors were "considering the possibility of saving the Michigan taxpayers some money by sending the killers to New York to burn." However, privately, he assured Ray and Martha that they would remain in Michigan.

"There won't be any attempt to extradite you," McMahon promised Martha, "and even if they try, I'll fight it. In fact, if they extradite you, I'll resign from my job as District Attorney that very day."

Martha's arched eyebrows showed her skepticism.

"You're sure that the statements I gave you won't be used against me?"

"I'll resign as Prosecuting Attorney of Kent County the day that you are taken out of the State to return to New York," McMahon pledged. "I'll swear on a Bible that as long as I am District Attorney you will never be removed from Kent County."

What McMahon left out of his assurances was that he opposed extradition of the pair only because he felt their death in the electric chair would be too painless. He believed they would be more properly punished for their crimes by spending the rest of their lives imprisoned in a Michigan penitentiary. The chances of that happening lessened when New York Governor Dewey signed extradition documents that very day.

With the death penalty now a very real possibility, Martha became more receptive to detectives as they tried to turn her and Ray against each other. Sensing that Martha was struggling with whether to confess, Sheriff Blacklock sought to plant a seed of mistrust toward her co-conspirator.

"For your own safety, in case Mr. McMahon loses his fight and you are returned to the State of New York, turn all of the blame over on Mr. Hernandez. Make it look like he is the one who killed Janet Fay, and not you."

She was especially receptive to the suggestions of Deputy Clarence Randle, who she viewed as a father figure. Randle revealed that Ray was ready to throw her under the bus. He told her that Ray "was planning on running out and leaving [her]" by fleeing the country alone, abandoning Martha to take the fall for their crimes:

Martha, we have talked to Ray and he has given us another statement in which he has pushed over all of the blame off on you. Don't be a sucker and take the blame for something that you can push off on somebody else. Make Ray share the blame with you because he has been lying to you all the time. We found a passport and one-way ticket to Spain with Ray's stuff. He was planning on leaving you behind.

To emphasize the point, he pulled out a photograph of Ray's wife, Encarnacion, and showed it to Martha. Martha studied the photo with stern, appraising eyes.

"This is the woman who kept me from marrying Ray," she seethed. "And I've even helped support her!"

With Martha visibly wavering in her loyalty to Ray, Randle delivered the final push needed to get her to turn on him.

"Ray has already told us that he was planning on killing you," Randle said.

Around 5:00 p.m. on March 3, McMahon informed Martha that "some authorities from New York" wanted to question her. He urged her to cooperate and answer their questions fully because it would get her a lighter sentence for the Downing murders. McMahon also assured her that he "told them the promise that I have made to you" about not being extradited to New York. Then he led her to another room where Edward Robinson, the Assistant District Attorney from Nassau County, New York, awaited her.

"Go in and cooperate with them and let him clear his records of the case in New York City," McMahon urged her.

After being introduced, Edward Robinson acknowledged the understanding that Martha would not be extradited, and he explained his reason for being there.

"Miss Beck, if it hadn't been for the promise that Roger McMahon has made for you, you might be transferred to New York to face the electric chair," Robinson told her. "I am here for the purpose of clearing up the records of the death of the woman in New York."

Martha gave a statement to Robinson recounting the same rendition of events that she had given to McMahon two days before. In detailing the murder of Janet Fay, Martha repeated that Ray had growled the command, "Get her quiet. I don't care how," and then hurried out of the room.

"Next thing I knew, I had the hammer in my hand and hit her,"

Martha calmly explained. "I hit her and she kind of fell sideways and was still moaning. I said, 'Ray!' and I hit her again."

When Ray came back into the room, Martha felt dazed and blankly uttered: "Look what I've done." Seeing Janet hunched over on the floor, Ray reacted instantly. He strode over to her and grabbed her by the throat.

"Still moaning?" asked Robinson, clarifying Janet's condition at the time.

"And groaning," Martha affirmed.

"Bleeding?"

"Terribly," she replied.

Like the crazed narrator of Poe's *The Tell Tale Heart* who thinks he hears his dead victim's heart beating, Martha resumed her macabre narrative:

> Then I put the scarf around her neck and we turned her over because at that time – I can still hear it! – the blood was dripping, dripping, dripping. I felt sure the people downstairs would hear the noise of the blood dripping from her head which was still resting on her suitcase. And the sound of it just sounded like it could be heard all over the house.

At that point in her statement, Martha picked up her handkerchief from the table, put a fountain pen in it, and turned her wrist to show how Ray had used the hammer and scarf as a tourniquet to strangle Janet.

Q. What did he do with the scarf then?

A. Tied it in a knot and put the end of the hammer in and kept twisting it.

Q. What did you think he was doing?

A. To keep her quiet as she was groaning.

Q. Did you realize what you were doing?

A. Certainly, we both realized then we had gone so far that we would have to –

Q. Kill her?

A. Yes.

Martha chain smoked as her description moved to the events surrounding the death of Rainelle Downing.

"That was hard," she said finally, "for I have two children of my own who are with my mother in Pensacola."

She also offered some insight into a possible motivation for Ray's behavior, sharing that Ray had confided to her that when he was 21-years-old, he "got into trouble over a woman. Some woman did him a mean turn...and he vowed to get revenge. Since then he had gotten even with more than 150 women."

Although investigators from numerous states suspected that Ray and Martha had killed in their jurisdictions, Martha insisted that the pair had only murdered Janet Fay, Deliphene Downing, and Rainelle Downing.

"If you bring me a Bible," Martha asserted, "I'll swear on it that there were only the three killed."

Not willing to take Martha's word for it, Roger McMahon encouraged investigators from other jurisdictions to review their missing persons cases and he requested the sheriff of Green Forest, Arkansas to investigate the death of Myrtle Young, including seeking exhumation of her body.

After finishing with Martha's statement, Edward Robinson took one from Ray as well. He covered much of the same information as Martha, but never made a proclamation or promise of only three murders. However, he did freely discuss details about his background, including how he had made Pearl Wilson move out of her daughter's New York apartment to go live with her son in Wilmington, North

Carolina. At the time, Robinson could not appreciate the irony of Ray's testimony about what had happened to Pearl's daughter, Jane Wilson Thompson.

Q. Was there an argument between you and Mrs. Wilson?

A. Not actually an argument...I was scared to have her stay. She was a sick woman and had to go to the doctor's twice every week.

Q. What connection did you have?

A. She was the mother of a girl I knew.

Q. A girl you had corresponded with?

A. Yes.

Q. Was she there also?

A. No, she died.

The next day, still separated from Ray, Martha wrote him a short letter, which Deputy Randle delivered to him:

Dearest Ray,

Just a note to let you know that I am okay and to tell you to please try not to worry too much. This would have happened sooner or later, so I guess it is for the best that it has happened.

My greatest desire is that you will not change in your thoughts toward me. But even though you do I will understand and it will never change my love for you. Nothing you do or say will make me love you less.

I have been told that before very long you and I will be permitted to see each other. I hope that you are being treated as nice as all the officers have been to me. They have been swell.

There is no reason why I should tell you that I love you – you know that. But, believe me, darling, no matter what the future holds in store for each of us I will love you until I die.

Please take care of yourself, Ray, and who knows, maybe we will be together again sometime. It may be when we are both old and gray, but even then you will still mean the same to me.

Remember, my dear, I love you more than anybody or anything in this world.

Yours forever,

Martha

As Martha was professing her everlasting love to Ray, friends and family of Deliphene Downing were attending her and Rainelle's dual funeral at the Methodist Church in Palisade, Nebraska, followed by their burial in Palisade Cemetery on a prairie near the farm where Deliphene played as a child. Mother and daughter shared a bronze-colored casket with Rainelle clasped in the left arm of her mother. They appeared to be sleeping peacefully, Deliphene wearing a French-blue dress and her daughter clad in a baby-blue velvet dress with a white lace collar. Baskets of hyacinths and daffodils adorned the top of the casket.

The Reverend John Denchfield, the same pastor who had presided over Deliphene's husband's funeral less than two years earlier, now oversaw the funeral for the remaining two members of the Downing family:

God forecast the deplorable depths to which man can sink and He sent His Son to live among men and attempt to redeem them. Christ was crucified as redemption for the sins of man. Despite this sacrifice, one murder is committed every 40 minutes throughout the world. Apparently, the teachings of Christ have not made an impression on the minds of men...Not even the dumbest animals stoop to such bestiality as has been shown here. It is beyond the compassion of any person with a natural Christian love to believe a fellow human being guilty of such vicious treatment of anyone, especially an innocent child.

Meanwhile, Ray penned a reply to Martha's message that had been hand delivered by Deputy Randle:

Dearest Martha,

I love you. I am being treated very well, with much respect. I miss you more than I ever dreamed I would. I am feeling much better after I have confessed everything. Also, I have been preparing to give my soul to God and I hope you will also pray and you will feel much better too.

I only hope that I get to see you again and be with you either here or in Heaven.

I love you so,

Ray

Chapter Fifteen

Early on the morning of March 8, two detectives came to Ray's cell in the Grand Rapids Jail. Each detective handcuffed him to one of their arms and they escorted him to a waiting car. Their destination was the capitol building in Lansing, Michigan. They were going to a hearing on the State of New York's motion to extradite Martha and Ray. Martha made the sixty-mile trip in a separate car.

A crowd of thousands of people awaited them outside the capitol building, spitting and cursing and booing the two murder suspects. The detectives transporting them had to push their way through the mob of people to enter the building. After getting inside, they led Ray and Martha to two separate rooms. Roger McMahon paid them both a visit before the hearing, reminding them that they did not need court appointed counsel because he would represent them: "I will defend you," he assured them.

In Governor G. Mennen Williams's chambers, Nassau County Assistant District Attorney Phillip Huntington presented a lengthy argument as to why Martha and Ray should be extradited to New York. Ray glanced at McMahon several times during Huntington's argument. McMahon smiled at him each time. After Huntington concluded,

McMahon stood up and, much to Ray's surprise, began his remarks by stating: "I recommend what Mr. Huntington has said."

———————

"I dropped almost dead at that time," Ray later recalled, having believed all of McMahon's promises that he would never support extradition.

———————

Led from Governor Williams's office after the hearing, a visibly deflated Martha told reporters: "I have seen the handwriting on the wall. I guess nothing can change it."

Ray projected a stoic calm. "They ought to kill me," he told reporters matter-of-factly. "I've done a terrible thing, but I'm not afraid of the chair. I guess that's the way I ought to die."

Later that day, he boasted about his success in seducing women.

"I have a way with women, a power over them. I guess I'm so attractive to members of the opposite sex because I'm actually a gentle person," he said with a straight face. "I pay them little attentions, little ones they all look for in a man. That's what makes them figure I'm sweet and lovable and kind. And in back of everything that's the way I am."

Around 9:00 p.m. that night, Ray was taken to a small, six-by-eight feet long room, where a man and woman were waiting. The man introduced himself as Adrian Verspoor, his court-appointed attorney.

"I think I have come a little bit too late," Verspoor told him. "I doubt I can do much at this point."

———————

On March 9, Michigan's Governor agreed to extradite Martha and Ray to New York under one important condition. In exchange for extradition of the pair, New York Governor Thomas Dewey would have to agree that they would be returned to Michigan if a first-degree murder conviction could not be obtained in New York. Already feeling political pressure, Dewey quickly assented. The New York public had made it perfectly clear that the highest penalty would have to be paid for the monstrous killing of Janet Fay.

Unnerved by news of the extradition and the now-looming specter of the death penalty, Martha paced back and forth in the narrow confines of her Grand Rapids jail cell.

"I don't want to go back to New York," she confessed to the matron guarding her. "I'm afraid of the electric chair."

During a jailhouse meeting the following day on March 11, Martha informed her court-appointed attorney, Adrian Verspoor, that she wanted to make a supplemental statement to detectives investigating the Janet Fay murder. The supplement was needed, she explained, to "correct" part of the statement that she had given eight days earlier. Verspoor strongly advised her not to speak further with investigators: "In my opinion, if you give this statement, you are placing yourself and Raymond guilty of first-degree murder in the State of New York," he said bluntly.

Martha understood Verspoor's warning, but she could not be dissuaded. She met again with Roger McMahon and went forward with making the supplemental statement, a statement which drastically changed the complexion of the case:

Q. Now, I understand also, there are some details with reference to the death of Mrs. Fay in New York that you hadn't told before, that you wish to tell at this time.

A. Yes, I would like to tell a little more. I would like to tell you about some things, Mr. McMahon, previous to this. I mean, I don't want you to think I am trying to slide out of this, but I just want to let you people know that all of this is not something that was created within me and I forced Ray to do it.

I am making a clean slate now and I would like to get everything that I know about right and everything that has come into this from the first time I met [Ray]. Really, I am trying to make my peace with God and I can't until I get it all off.

She sought to unburden her heart. She wanted to relieve her guilty conscious by giving the true version of events that occurred during the predawn hours of February 1.

In going back to the night of Mrs. Fay's death. It is hard to sit here and know by telling those words I am just signing my own death warrant, but down deep in my heart I feel I can't do anything else but tell the exact truth. Well, the first part of my confession you have it correct as to the way that Ray got her name on the paper and the signing of the checks and all. There is only one part that is wrong and it is wrong in one sense of the word and the other part of that is right. The part about the hammer. While I was washing dishes, Ray went down and got the hammer out of the trunk of the car and wrapped it in a newspaper, brought it back and put it up on the icebox. I said, "Ray, what is that for?" He said, "We may have trouble tonight and have to use it."

Next morning, she got up and went over to get her clothes to dress and Ray motioned to the kitchen and did like that [indicating] and I took it for granted that he motioned for me to go and get the hammer which I did and brought it back. I had on a housecoat and I held the hammer in my sleeve next to my arm. Then I went in and held it out to Ray and he said "No, you have got to do it." I said, "I can't." We were saying it very low because she was talking then as to getting out of the house. He said, "You have got to do it" and I said, "I can't." He said, "If you love me you will do it. Now."

That is when I hit her.

Martha added that after striking Janet with the hammer once in the head, she stopped and looked at Ray and murmured his name. She only delivered the second blow after he directed: "Hit her again."

Told about Martha's new statement, Ray could not believe his ears.

She was now admitting that the murder of Janet Fay was much more of a premeditated act than their prior statements had characterized it, and she was shifting much of the blame to him.

"She must be mentally unbalanced if she said such a thing," he told McMahon.

Chapter Sixteen

A few days after Martha's supplemental statement, she and Ray boarded a plane bound for New York. They landed at New York's La Guardia airport just before 3:00 p.m. on March 15. Awaiting the plane at Gate 6-A were Nassau District Attorney James Gehrig, Nassau Head Detective Stuyvesant Pinnell, four other Nassau detectives, and additional New York police. A crowd of several hundred spectators who had also gathered at the gate that cold afternoon watched as the well-dressed, but tired-looking pair emerged from the plane with their police escorts and descended the mobile stairs to the ground.

Already anticipating that Ray and Martha would seek to use a defense of insanity at trial, District Attorney Gehrig retained medical experts Perry Lichtenstein and James McCartney to aid the prosecution. The two psychiatrists were specifically instructed to build a rebuttal to the expected insanity plea of *"foile a deux,"* or "madness of two," a shared psychotic condition in which two people – though each individually sane – inspire each other to madness by the nature of their relationship.

A novel basis for mounting a defense in legal proceedings, the theory of *foile a deux* asserts the transmission of delusions, by the "inducer" who suffers from a psychotic disorder, to another person who may share the inducer's delusions in entirety or in part. Famed defense attorney Clarence Darrow had unsuccessfully pleaded *foile a deux* in defense of Nathan Leopold and Richard Loeb in the Bobby Franks murder case in Chicago in 1924. In that case, defense psychiatrists deemed Loeb the inducer and Leopold his "emotional slave."

Gehrig suspected that defense counsel would attempt to cast Martha as the emotional slave in her relationship with Ray. To be prepared to undercut a *foile a deux* defense, Lichenstein and McCartney were on hand at the airport to observe the pair and assess the extent to which Martha fell under some of the condition's key risk factors, including her female gender, suggestibility, passivity, histrionic personality traits, suspiciousness, and dependency. They watched closely as Martha stepped off the plane wearing a "full-length Persian lamb coat" and a blue hat with a veil "tied cutely around her expansive chin." Martha's choice of attire contrasted with Ray's conservative, neutral colored suit. The state's psychiatrists did not have a chance to observe much more than that as Ray and Martha were quickly whisked away from the landing site and taken to police headquarters in Mineola, where they were formally booked at 4:15 following some preliminary questioning by investigators. Less than an hour later, Martha was transported to her new residence in the House of Detention for Women at 10th Street and Greenwich Avenue, while Ray was taken to his new home in the Bronx County Jail.

A matron who tended to Martha in the detention house was surprised to find that she actually took a liking to her:

> When I went in to talk to Martha the first time, I guess I felt like anyone would – that a woman who'd kill a kid – well, nothing was bad enough for her. But pretty soon I began to forget what she'd done and, in spite of myself, I began to like her. Why? This sounds funny, I know, but there was something genuinely humble about her, a pathetic eagerness to please. She was childlike...she had a tremendously vivacious personality, but again it was a child's personality.

Subsequent psychiatric evaluations by Lichtenstein and McCartney found that Martha's emotional growth stopped when she was eight or nine years old, while Ray exhibited a "lack of conscience." Ray understood the "horror of his deeds," but rationalized his criminal conduct to such a degree that he "seemed to suffer no slightest pang of guilt or remorse." Consistent with the state's depiction of him as "diabolically clever and always calculating," Ray scored a 135 on his IQ test, close to the borderline of genius. The State's psychiatric report on Martha included the conclusion:

We believe that, at most, she is a psychopathic personality. This is based on the following:

– Her promiscuous and perverted relationship with the codefendant.

– Her willingness to discard her children just so she could obtain the love of Fernandez.

– Her two attempts at suicide.

– Her continued association with the codefendant even though she knew he was married, and her participation in his original activities.

Momentarily reunited on March 21, Ray and Martha held hands for two hours across the table in a conference room in Nassau County Jail while meeting with Herbert Rosenberg, the young Manhattan attorney retained by Martha's family to represent her and appointed by the court to represent Ray at his request. Only thirty-nine, Rosenberg had served as a first lieutenant in the military police prior to becoming a lawyer. Though new to the law, he already had a reputation for zealously representing his clients. Afterward, guards allowed Ray and Martha a quick kiss on their way back to their cells at opposite ends of the jail.

The next day, prosecutors filed a formal indictment against the

Lonely Hearts Killers, alleging that on January 4, 1949, Ray and Martha *each then and there aiding and abetting the other, willfully, feloniously, and of malice aforethought, killed one Janet J. Fay.* Martha "smiled and waved at the crowd" as she entered Nassau County Court for her arraignment. In response to the court clerk's inquiry as to how she pleaded to the indictment of murdering Janet Fay, Martha replied "not guilty by reason of insanity" in what an observer described as a "clear, carrying voice." Ray simply replied "the same" when the clerk addressed him.

Ray and Martha shared a passionate kiss in the courtroom corridor afterward.

"Don't worry, darling," Ray assured her. "We'll be together again soon. After the trial we'll go to Niagara Falls on our honeymoon."

Martha reached up with her unrestrained hand and straightened his tie.

"I'm looking forward to it," she said with a radiant smile.

Handcuffed to a deputy by her right wrist, Martha put her left arm around the back of Ray's neck and tilted her head down to Ray's lips while a group of deputies and attorneys looked on with nervous smiles. The kiss continued until the guard handcuffed to Ray's right arm forcibly pulled him away.

By strange coincidence, during his representation of the Lonely Hearts killers, Herbert Rosenberg experienced his own version of the loneliness of a damaged relationship. His "pretty brunette" wife of three years, 26-year-old Rosemary Kraemer Rosenberg, separated from him and moved back to her parents' home in California. Ironically, Rosenberg had obtained a divorce for Rosemary from her first husband in July 1946 and then married her himself the very next day.

Although she often appeared untroubled and upbeat in public at court appearances, some evidence suggests that Martha may have been haunted by what she did while under Ray's influence. She was inadvertently tormented by one of the prison matrons assigned to watch her cell because of the matron's physical resemblance to one of Martha's victims. Mrs. Augusta Carlson so resembled Janet Fay that Martha could not bear to look at her and Herbert Rosenberg reported to jail officials that she was "on the verge of committing violence." To defuse the situation, Mrs. Carlson resigned from her position on April 7.

"I had no idea that I looked like Mrs. Fay," Carlson told reporters. "I feel sorry for Mrs. Beck and would rather quit than make her feel bad."

On May 12, Judge Thomas Cuff granted the defendants' Motion for Change of Venue, moving the trial from Nassau County to Bronx County on grounds that the "atmosphere of Nassau County has been so thoroughly charged with prejudice against them by reason of articles appearing in the local daily newspapers that they cannot expect a fair trial in that county." In support of the motion, Rosenberg included two affidavits from private investigators who swore they canvassed residents of Nassau County and found the "overwhelming opinion" of the public to be that Ray and Martha "deserve to be electrocuted" without the need for a trial.

Meanwhile, the pressures of the justice system began to get to Ray.

"I want my freedom," he screamed while being led into the courtroom for one of the countless pretrial hearings requested by the parties' attorneys as they prepared for trial. "I want justice!"

He brushed aside photographers' requests that he kiss Martha, responding with an indignant "No, I'll wait until later when I have more time, and I'll have plenty of time."

Then he turned toward Martha, his eyes at once both angry and tender.

"Honey, I love you," he told her with an affectionate smile. "That's all I can say. I know we are innocent."

Chapter Seventeen

Amidst heavy news coverage of their arrests and the allegations of their crimes, the Lonely Hearts Killers gained national notoriety. There was widespread public interest in the case of the "marry-for-murder pair" and "kiss-and-kill sweethearts" as it went to trial. The trial took place on the sixth floor of the Bronx County Court House, a twelve-story, steel-framed structure clad in limestone and resting on a granite platform with Classical style columns marking the building's entrances. Built between 1931 and 1934 during the Great Depression, the imposing courthouse dwarfed nearby buildings and stood practically within shouting distance of historic Yankee Stadium.

Jury selection began on June 6 with Judge Ferdinand Pecora presiding. Held in high esteem among members of the judiciary and bar, Judge Pecora was a "small, swarthy" man with a reputation as a stern but fair judge. A fellow judge summed up Pecora's high regard for justice with the observation that "To Pecora, the pedestal on which he stands is more important than his pocketbook." Born in Sicily, Judge Pecora shared part of Raymond Fernandez's background in having been forced to leave school as a teenager, but unlike Ray he eventually returned to academics and worked his way through law school. Pecora became famous in the 1930's representing the United

States Senate Committee on Banking and Currency during its investigation of Wall Street banking and stock brokerage practices that preceded the Stock Market Crash of 1929. The irregular practices that Pecora's probe exposed had improperly benefited the upper class to the detriment of ordinary investors. Pecora took great pride in having helped expose the shady trading practices and his investigation led to major reforms in the American financial system.

By the end of the first day of trial, only one juror had been picked from the jury pool of 450 talesmen: Fred Yobs, an accountant who automatically became foreman of the jury as the first member selected. The process of questioning prospective jurors, challenging them for cause, and selecting or striking them via peremptory challenge continued to drag on as the days turned into weeks. Defense attorney Herbert Rosenberg, who faced the "herculean task" of representing both defendants, spent hour after hour asking jury pool members about their views toward his clients. He focused much of his time inquiring about sexual issues pertinent to the case, such as asking prospective jurors if they would be prejudiced to learn that Ray and Martha had "unusual sexual habits" and if women jurors would be embarrassed sitting with men jurors if "certain lurid details as to sex" were testified about.

"Would the fact that Mrs. Beck loves Mr. Fernandez prejudice you in any way?" Rosenberg asked a prospective male juror. Martha smiled when the man answered "No."

All of the focus on his sex life seemed to strike a nerve in Ray. On the tenth day of jury selection, Rosenberg asked prospective jurors whether they would be prejudiced against the defendants if "it develops that Fernandez met many ladies through lonely hearts clubs and had dealings with them, sexual or otherwise." When Rosenberg repeatedly rephrased the question to one juror in particular, Ray leaped to his feet and hurled a pencil across the glass-top defense table.

"I object! That's enough!" he shouted at Rosenberg, pounding his fist onto the table. "You mentioned all that before! That's enough, I say!" he bellowed, his face blazing with rage.

Silence engulfed the courtroom as a bailiff grasped Ray's shoulder and forced him back into his chair. Red-faced after the outburst, Rosenberg requested a recess, which the judge denied, but after briefly conferring with his clients, Rosenberg continued the line of questioning. By the end of the day, no new jurors were chosen.

Finally, after twelve days of jury selection, a full twelve-member jury was empaneled. Culled from three panels totaling more than 600 veniremen, the jury ultimately comprised ten men and two women, the men mostly clerks or accountants, the two women both housewives.

Judge Pecora scheduled the next phase of the trial for June 27. Hoping to hear opening statements from the attorneys for both sides, crowds of curious people passed through the arched marble entrances to the courthouse lobby. A throng of people filled the wood paneled courtroom and spilled outside into the corridor. Record heat that summer made the large crowd particularly impressive, and the crowds continued throughout the trial in spite of the oppressive heat that included a trio of three-day heat waves in less than a six-week period in July and August with temperatures in New York City hitting 99-102-95 on July 3-5, 97-99-95 on July 28-30, and 100-98-99 on August 9-11. The record heat even reached the northern part of the state where five, four, and three-day heat waves scorched Albany from late June to August. Without central air conditioning, sitting in a packed, stuffy courtroom was not a comfortable way to spend the summer. But not even the miserable conditions kept the curious away from the spectacle of the trial. Newspaper stories had hinted at Ray and Martha's depraved sexual practices and now the public wanted to hear all of the sordid details. Alfred Kinsey's book, *Sexual Behavior in the Human Male*, had been published just the year before, causing widespread controversy with its findings challenging conventional beliefs about sexuality and its discussion of subjects previously considered taboo. Now the trial of the Lonely Hearts Killers promised to go even further with first-hand accounts of sexual acts formerly shunned as unspeakable.

At 10:30 a.m., Assistant District Attorney Edward Robinson stood up from the prosecution table and promised the jury that the evidence would show Janet Fay's murder had been a premeditated act by Ray and Martha. When his comments came to the facts of the murder itself, Robinson described how Martha hit Janet twice in the head with a hammer, and then, as Janet "lay moaning and crying and bleeding on the floor," Ray wrapped a scarf around her neck, tied a knot in the scarf, and inserted the handle of the hammer into the knot. He turned the handle "as you would a tourniquet, very hard, fast and tight, against the neck until there was no more moaning, no more groaning, and no more life." Robinson twisted his hands to dramatize how the tight turning had fractured Janet's larynx and choked her to death.

When his turn came to address the jury, Herbert Rosenberg spent much of the time pointing out what he deemed overzealousness on the part of the prosecution.

"I will show you folks that the District Attorney who is sitting here is electric-chair-minded and a conviction-happy district attorney," Rosenberg emphasized. "I will show vindictiveness and desire upon the district attorney of Nassau County to burn the defendants."

Perhaps foreshadowing a plea of *foile a deux*, he also told the jury that the crime charged would fall under the definition of manslaughter as an unintentional killing, rather than a premeditated murder.

"The defendants became so involved sexually that it was impossible for them to act as normal individuals," Rosenberg asserted, adding that because of Martha's emotional and sexual attachment to Ray, she could not distinguish right from wrong at the time. Rosenberg's opening statement suggested that the defense strategy would be that Martha was legally insane when Janet died and that since Ray had no foreknowledge of the crime, he should be guilty only as an accessory after the fact.

Through the first days of the trial, Ray and Martha had talked affectionately to each other across the defense table, laughing at times in response to something the other said. Dorothy Kilgallen, observing the trial for the *New York Journal-American*, noted how at ease they seemed, particularly Martha, who she described as "serene" and "cool as a cucumber," while "every recess sees her jogging out the courtroom with bounce in her step and a laugh on her lips."

But before long Martha began to show signs of stress from being on trial in the shadow of the electric chair. On one of the first days of witness testimony, Anna Arnsperger, owner of the Valley Stream apartment-home in which Janet Fay was murdered, testified that a few days after January 3, she saw Ray and Martha take a trunk out of the apartment and put it into their car.

Upon hearing Arnsperger's testimony, Martha glared at her and growled: "Are you being paid to sit there and tell such lies like that?"

After Justice Ferdinand Pecora admonished her to be silent, Martha sneered in a spiteful voice still loud enough for the visibly shaken witness to hear: "She's telling such lies, she must be getting paid."

During direct examination of Nassau County Detective Charles Hildebrandt, prosecutors dramatically brandished the blood-stained Ballpein hammer that had been recovered from a toolbox in Ray's car after his arrest. Detective Hildebrandt testified that while Martha was being held in Michigan, she identified the hammer as belonging to Ray and while she could not say for sure that it was the actual murder weapon, she did confirm that it was "like the one" used to kill Janet Fay. Although Martha and Ray had displayed confident smiles for most of the day, the appearance of the hammer noticeably darkened their mood.

Later, during cross examination of Detective John Vander Band, defense attorney Rosenberg sought to show the jury that the confessions given by Ray and Martha had been effectively coerced.

"Prior to the supplemental statement given by Mrs. Beck on March 11, did she ever comment that you were trying to bully her?"

"I can't recall sir," the detective replied curtly. "But it's not my policy to offend anyone."

"Did Mr. Fernandez ever say to you: 'Let me alone. I'll say anything you want. I've had no sleep?'"

"No," Vander Band insisted, while admitting that Ray had "said he was tired several times during the investigation."

The jury seemed bored for much of the cross-examination, as Vander Band blandly responded to most of Rosenberg's questions with

"I don't recall" or "I can't recall that." However, the detective conceded that Ray told him he would back Martha "100 per cent because he loved her," an acknowledgement Rosenberg hoped would sway the jury into believing Ray's contention that he had lied in his confessions.

Chapter Eighteen

On the afternoon of July 12, Ray took the witness stand becoming the eighth defense witness on the twenty-sixth day of trial. Throughout the trial, he had been receiving regular fan mail from women interested in a romantic relationship, some of them even proposing marriage. But this was his chance to tell the whole world his story.

In a soft, suave voice, often pausing to look over and smile at Martha, he explained how he began using the name "Charles Martin" in 1946 or 1947 in various lonely hearts clubs correspondence, before going on to describe what he referred to as the "occurrence of Mrs. Janet Fay." He flatly denied killing Janet Fay or planning to kill her, testifying instead that he had lied to District Attorney Edward Robinson in his original statement given on March 3 in an attempt to protect Martha. He said he told Robinson that he had hit Janet Fay with a hammer because investigators convinced him to protect Martha by taking the blame because "it would give her a chance for her freedom."

Although he had confessed in Michigan shortly after his arrest that Janet Fay was still moaning when he and Martha put a scarf around her neck, the story changed during Ray's testimony at trial. He continued backpedaling from the original statement he had given to detectives shortly after his arrest by testifying at trial that he had lied about the fact that Janet was still moaning when he tied a scarf as a tourniquet around her neck. He also denied putting a hammer handle into the scarf and tightening it around Janet's neck. The scarf was not to kill her, Ray explained, but to stop her from bleeding: "As I put her body on the floor, blood started gushing out of her head and to stop that bleeding so it wouldn't get all over the place in handling her, I put a scarf around her neck to try to stop the flow of blood."

Rosenberg wanted him to explain why his story changed.

Q. Did you tell any lies?

A. I told many.

Q. Why did you tell lies?

A. They promised me or they told me or even begged me, as you may say, that for Martha's sake, being a woman and having children, that I could give her an opportunity by taking the blame, certain blames, saying things different ways, and make it look like myself was the murderer; it was on my fault and the case was in my hands; that Mrs. Fay's death was caused by my hand instead of hers.

.....

They told me what Martha was saying and even asked if it was true what she had said. I told them it was lies...They told me I should agree with her to help her. After all, since I was never going to leave the prison, I should take all the blame and give her a chance for her freedom, which I did.

.....

Q. And even if it was a lie you were willing to help her, is that correct?

A. Yes; anything.

"All of my statements were made for the purpose of helping Martha," he stated like the Spanish gentleman he believed himself to be. "I love her," he said gallantly, all the while gazing at her with gentle, adoring eyes. "It couldn't be anything else."

Asked about the hammer that Martha used to hit Janet, Ray denied going downstairs the night of the murder to get it out of the trunk of his car. He also categorically denied ever having commanded, suggested, or requested Martha to use the hammer, a common "household hammer," against Janet.

Q. Around 9 o'clock that evening did you ever tell the defendant Beck or anybody else that you may have trouble and have to use that hammer?

A. I never did such a thing.

Q. Did the defendant Beck ever hold a hammer out to you and you said no, she has to use the hammer?

A. No.

Q. Did you ever say to the defendant Beck that "You have got to do it" and that you could not do it?

A. Do what?

Q. That she would have to do it and that you could not use the hammer?

A. Well, no.

Q. Did you ever tell the defendant Beck that if she loved you she would use the hammer?

A. No.

Ray also asserted that he would never have confessed to the Janet Fay murder but for District Attorney Robinson's promise that he and Martha would stay in Michigan for life and not be extradited to New York to face the death penalty. Rosenberg attempted to elicit testimony establishing that the governors of Michigan and New York entered into an agreement whereby Ray and Martha would be extradited to New York to face the death penalty for killing Janet Fay, but would be sent back to Michigan to be tried for the murders of Deliphene and Rainelle Downing if they were not convicted in New York. However, Judge Pecora refused to allow any evidence of the "Governors Agreement" because he concluded that such an agreement "has nothing to do with this case." Despite the judge's ruling, Rosenberg refused to back down about the matter.

> Court: I have said before, I say it again, that that has nothing to do with the trial of this case.
>
> Rosenberg: Do you know what will happen to you if you are acquitted here, Mr. Fernandez?
>
> Robinson: Objected to, if the Court please, improper.
>
> Court: Sustained. Now, if you are seeking to circumvent my ruling about the so-called Governors' agreement, I am cautioning you not to do it.
>
> Rosenberg: If your Honor please, I am trying to protect the rights of my client who is now testifying.
>
> Court: You will not protect the rights of this client in defiance of my rulings!
>
> .....

Rosenberg: If your Honor please, I object to the way – I even object to the way your Honor raises your voice.

Court: I raised my voice in order to impress you, if possible, with what I have been trying to impress you with so many times.

Rosenberg: Your Honor does not have to raise your voice to impress me. Your Honor can rule on an objection. You don't have to raise –

Court: Don't tell me what tone of voice I must use!

Rosenberg's persistence in pursuing the matter became a point of contention with the court, creating an antagonism between the defense attorney and judge that would continue throughout the course of the trial.

Chapter Nineteen

The ongoing media circus covering the trial ensured that Judge Pecora's courtroom stayed packed with spectators throughout the colorful proceedings, but July 20 proved to be an especially popular day of the trial. In an effort to bolster their insanity defense, Herbert Rosenberg steered his direct examination of Ray to detail the "abnormal" sexual practices that Ray and Martha shared during their rocky romance. After a lunch-time recess, a line of women stretched outside the courtroom doors, and at least thirty were turned away due to lack of seats. At one point, the mob of spectators grew so large that ten additional police had to be summoned from the nearby Highbridge Police Station to help the regular court deputies with crowd control.

With the courtroom "crowded with women," Ray's testimony about unusual sex acts caused three women jurors to close their eyes and shield their faces with their hands, and the scandalous details sent one female spectator fleeing from the room. Rosenberg asked Ray about Martha's visit to a "Latin doctor" practicing in the building next to Ray's apartment on 139th Street, from whom Martha had sought help in achieving sexual satisfaction.

"She told me that never in her life had she enjoyed sexual intercourse," Ray testified. "I had sent her to the doctor. I had bought her medicines, and what else could I do? She wouldn't answer, and I said, 'What has the doctor told you? But she wouldn't answer me."

Members of the public watching the trial from the courtroom gallery hung on every word as Ray recounted how Martha had told him that the doctor suggested they try cunnilingus. Before continuing with more details, Ray glanced at Martha as if to make sure it was okay. He proceeded only after she nodded her consent.

"I got down in between her legs, as we call it, her vagina, and I put my tongue to it." Ray said. "She enjoyed it. Before I had finished, she gave a screech and got frenetic and told me that was the first time she ever received such a thing."

He repeated the process the next day, but this time she reciprocated by giving him fellatio at the same time. The candid disclosure of intimately sexual acts shocked and fascinated the jury and other men and women in the courtroom gallery. It was an alien language to their Puritan ears.

During cross examination, District Attorney Robinson sharply questioned Ray about Jane Thompson, Deliphene Downing, Myrtle Young, and Esther Henne, repeatedly raising his voice and challenging Ray's answers during the withering interrogation. Frustrated by the hostile questioning, Ray shouted back at Robinson and nervously twisted a pencil in his hands. Asked about Henne, the lone survivor of the four, Ray smugly asserted that she had left him over a lack of sexual attention.

"It was because I ignored her sexually," he said, basking in Martha's obvious approval. "I ignored her completely in sexual relations."

During re-direct examination, Ray again denied ever planning on killing Janet Fay, insisting there was no reason to murder her since he had already succeeded in swindling her out of her money.

Q. You hadn't planned to kill her then?

A. There was no reason to, I had the money in my pocket already...If I could get some money from her, that was my plan.

Q. That was the same plan you followed with these other women that you mentioned?

A. The same thing.

....

Q. What were your intentions with respect to Mrs. Fay?

A. My intentions were to draw her away from her family, to pull her away till I could get some money from her and then send her back to Albany.

He claimed that Janet had been coming on to him throughout the night of January 3 and that he had grown increasingly agitated about it until he eventually told Martha: "Quiet that woman, I don't care how," before going into the bathroom for a few minutes. While still in the bathroom, he heard Martha yell his name, and when he rushed back into the living room, he saw Martha standing between the couch and armchair. Clad in a pink chenille bathrobe, Janet lay motionless, slumped over her suitcase.

"There appeared to be blood all over the floor, all surrounding her, and everything," he told the transfixed courtroom.

Spectators in the courtroom gallery gasped as he described the ghastly scene. His testimony took the jury back to the night of January 3:

Mrs. Fay was crouched over a suitcase. I saw her head was all splattered with blood. The suitcase was full of blood. On the floor was a great puddle of blood. I rushed over to Mrs. Beck. She was standing straight just looking down at Mrs. Fay and no movement, she didn't say a word.

I shook her and I said: "Martha, has happened? She came out of something like a daze – I don't know if it was a daze or coma, whatever it was, and she looked down and she says: "My God!" She says: "What has happened?"

I said: "You ought to know better than I do." She got on her knees and took her pulse...and told me: "It's too late. There is nothing we can do for her. She's dead."

Asked to explain why he had tied a scarf around Janet's throat, Ray insisted that he did so simply to stop her neck from bleeding. He denied harming Janet in any way, either before Martha struck her with the hammer or afterward.

Q. Did you ever strangle Mrs. Fay?

A. You can't strangle a dead body...She was dead before I put the scarf around her.

On further questioning, Ray contradicted statements that Martha had made to detectives during the first few days following their arrests, again insisting that the statements he made to detectives during the first few days in custody had been falsified to protect Martha from the death penalty. His love for her had compelled him to lie for her, and he swore that he would still do anything to shield her from harm.

Q. Would you be willing to go to the electric chair to spare the life of the defendant Beck?

A: I will volunteer for that.

Revisiting the night of Janet Fay's murder, Ray testified that Janet was worried about her money and wanted reassurance that it was safe. In this version of events, when Ray confirmed that the funds were safe and secure, Janet told him that she really just wanted to be near him. He could smell fresh perfume on her and noticed newly applied makeup. He could tell that she "wanted caressing, so I left because I was in no mood for it." When he came out of the bedroom after talking to Martha, Janet was "slouched over the suitcase" with "blood all over her head."

During further cross-examination, Robinson sought to establish a motive for Janet Fay's murder that contradicted Ray's insistence that he had no reason to kill her once he had conned her out of her money.

Q. Had she complained about the money before she went to bed?

A. She never complained about the money until that morning, Mr. Robinson.

Q. And that was just before she was killed, wasn't it?

A. That is true.

Martha sat attentively as her lover testified, occasionally smiling at him and scribbling notes on a legal pad. Her three older sisters, all dressed in "funeral black," sat in the front row sobbing from time to time with their mother. During a break in the proceedings, Martha turned to her sisters and smiled. "Don't cry," she said, despite her own sadness clearly evident in her voice.

Meanwhile, the earlier friction between Herbert Rosenberg and Judge Pecora continued as the defendants' counsel attempted to introduce evidence of deceptive practices on the part of investigators in inducing Ray and Martha to make statements against their interests shortly after their arrests. Just minutes after the morning session of trial began, the judge and defense counsel had another heated exchange about the extradition agreement between Michigan and New York:

Court: Mr. Rosenberg, let me remind you that I have repeatedly ruled throughout this trial that the agreement to which you have referenced has no relevancy to this trial.

Rosenberg: I respectfully submit it has great relevancy to the –

Court: I have already ruled against you, not once but many times, on that question.

Rosenberg: I take exception to your Honor's ruling.

Court: Take your exception and do not refer to the subject again, because it is not relevant.

Rosenberg: It is my intention to show it is relevant, Judge.

Court: I have ruled against you, Mr. Rosenberg, and I do not want to have to make the ruling again. If you insist on it, I may have to regard your conduct as contumacious. Now proceed.

Rosenberg: I make the same objection to your Honor's remark. Do I understand from your Honor that I may not mention that agreement even when I put the defendant Beck on the stand?

Court: If you do not understand my ruling, then either you are deficient in your knowledge of English or I am.

It was now clear – if it had not been before – that Herbert Rosenberg had an uphill battle on his hands in trying to save Ray and Martha from the electric chair.

After completing his redirect examination of Ray, Rosenberg recalled him to elicit testimony about the circumstances under which he had given his March 3 statement to investigators while being held in Michigan. He hoped to bring into evidence the fact that Ray had been induced into confessing to the murder of Deliphene Downing by representations from Michigan authorities that he would not face the death penalty and would instead serve a life sentence there. Judge Pecora refused to allow the line of questioning, ruling that the Michigan case had no relevancy to the trial about Janet Fay's murder in New York.

Perhaps frustrated and trying to get around the judge's ruling, Rosenberg asked an odd question given that it would not paint his client in a very good light in the eyes of the jury. Indeed, the question invited evidence of another serious crime, something a defense attorney would typically prefer not being injected into the trial.

"Isn't it a fact, Mr. Fernandez, that you pleaded guilty to shooting and killing a person in the State of Michigan in a court in the State of Michigan?"

"I did," Ray testified in reply.

The door opened, Judge Pecora asked for clarification.

"Is that for the shooting and killing of Mrs. Downing that you refer to?"

"Yes, sir," Ray replied.

Rosenberg's final question for Ray shed some light on his strategy.

"Mr. Fernandez, did you kill Janet Fay?" he asked.

"No," Ray said, his face the model of sincerity.

It seemed Rosenberg hoped that Ray's admission of guilt of another capital offense would boost his credibility in the minds of the jurors with respect to his denial of guilt for the murder of Janet Fay.

Following Ray's testimony, the judge admitted his March 3 statement to Michigan authorities into evidence, along with Martha's statement from the same date and her supplemental statement from March 11. All three statements were read into the record in their entirety by District Attorney Robinson. With the admission of their three prior statements, the credibility of the defendants became of paramount importance. They needed the jury to believe that the true version of events could be found solely in the testimony they were giving under oath at trial.

Rosenberg had yet to put his star witness on the stand, but Martha's time to testify grew closer. While she listened to Ray's testimony and awaited her turn in the spotlight, she smiled from time to time having apparently regained her peaceful demeanor, seemingly once again at ease with the situation. Her calm composure left a lasting impact on reporter Dorothy Kilgallen as she continued to cover the trial. Kilgallen was especially struck by Martha's hands:

It is her hands that really tell the story of her calm. They lie, one in her lap, one on the table in front of her, absolutely relaxed, the fingers curled a little like a child's...and they look gentle. If these are the hands that wielded the hammer that cracked the skull of the widow named Janet Fay...then someone should take a picture of them for the annals of crime and criminals.

She and other observers struggled to understand how such gentle, childlike hands had not only brutally taken the life of Janet Fay, but had also extinguished the life of Rainelle Downing, an innocent child not even three-years-old.

Chapter Twenty

D espite the scorching hot summer days, the public's appetite for details about the Lonely Hearts Killers remained insatiable. Demand for seats inside the courtroom grew so strong that, as *The New York Times* observed, "unauthorized persons were not permitted to loiter outside the courtroom" and "many of the would-be spectators, predominately women, did without lunch in order not to lose their places." The trial was already a nationwide sensation, but as much as the public's attention had been riveted by Ray's account of Janet Fay's murder and the "abnormal" sexual practices of his strange romance with Martha, they wanted to hear what Martha had to say even more. Dorothy Kilgallen reflected the general expectation that her testimony "will be something straight out of the Kinsey report." The excitement reached such a fever pitch that Judge Pecora had to quell a "riotous demonstration when 150 persons, mostly middle-aged women, tried to rush the courtroom." He ordered that the courtroom doors be locked and the corridors be cleared of the curious women and men eager to witness the proceedings.

Anticipation levels for Martha's testimony had been growing exponentially for weeks, so when defense attorney Herbert Rosenberg at long-last called her to testify on July 25 a collective hush came over the crowded courtroom. All eyes in the room watched expectantly as Martha, wearing a gray and white polka dot summer dress accented with two strands of pearls, slowly stood up at the defense table. But rather than going directly to the witness stand, she took a little detour, making her way to the other end of the table where Ray sat. Leaning slightly forward, she pulled his face gently toward her and planted a passionate kiss on his mouth. Sporting a smudge of red lipstick, Ray grinned in amusement as Martha strutted her way to the witness stand "with a Mona Lisa smile."

Rosenberg wasted no time getting to the thrust of his defense strategy. From the outset of his direct examination of Martha, he structured his questioning to show that she was so affected by her love for Ray that she was not in her right mind at the time of Janet Fay's murder.

Q. Did you kill Janet Fay?

A. I don't know.

Q. Were you in love with anybody on the 4th day of January 1949, the date of the alleged killing?

A. Yes, sir.

Q. Will you state to this Court and jury who you were in love with and who you are in love with today?

A. I loved, I do love, and I will always love Raymond Fernandez.

Like Ray, Martha backtracked from the statements she had given in Michigan back in March. Holding "her head high" and speaking in a "soft voice," Martha claimed that she "told more lies than the truth" in the statements she had previously given to Roger McMahon. "I was laughing to myself at the number of lies I had told him," she said.

To support a defense that she had a "fanatical and abnormal attachment" to Ray and that a "covetous, mad jealousy" deprived her of reason, Martha asserted that in the moments leading up to Janet Fay's murder, Janet had become sexually aggressive towards Ray and when Martha confronted her about it, Janet slapped her in the face. After the slap, Martha blacked out and when she came to, she was standing over Janet's body clutching a blood-stained hammer in her hand.

The details of Martha's version of the murder differed from Ray's account. Martha testified that she, Ray, and Janet went to bed at midnight on January 3. Around 3:30 a.m., Janet woke Martha from a sound sleep and went into the living room. Shortly afterward, Ray came into the bedroom and complained that Janet was bothering him. He told Martha to "talk to her and bring her back to bed." While Ray went to the bathroom, Martha walked into the living room and saw Janet on the couch.

Q. And how was she dressed?

A. She was completely nude.

Q. What did you say when you entered that room?

A. When I walked to the door there and I looked in and saw her in that position and in the nude, I says, "My gosh, Janet, what do you think you're doing?" She jumped up. She picked up her gown that was lying on the floor in front of the couch and she slipped that over her head and put the robe on and she says: "I wasn't expecting you."

Q. What did you say to her then?

A. I said: "I can see that by your appearance, that you certainly wasn't." I said: "What do you think you're doing?" She says, "Well, I was expecting Ray to come in the door." And I said, "For a woman of your age, you're the hottest bitch that I have ever seen." When I said that, she rushed over towards me and drew back her fist and slapped me.

.....

Q. What is the next thing you recall?

A. The next thing I know, Raymond had me by the shoulder . . . and was shaking me.

Q. Where was Mrs. Fay when you first saw her after you realized that Fernandez was shaking you by the shoulders?

A. She was slumped over a suitcase at my feet.

Q. Did you observe her physical condition?

A. She was lying there motionless.

Q. Did you observe any appearance of blood?

A. I took in everything at once. There appeared to be blood all over the floor, all surrounding her, and everything.

Playing the part of the dutiful, obedient lover, Martha told the jury that even though she could not remember killing Janet Fay, she would have done anything for Ray.

"I was so attached to Mr. Fernandez by that time, my love for him was so great, that if he had told me to hold my breath and stop breathing, I would have done it."

Chapter Twenty-One

Rosenberg devoted a substantial portion of Martha's direct examination to familiarizing the jury with her background. He wanted to be sure that the jurors were aware of experiences and events that would support an insanity defense. During her testimony, Martha wore heavy make-up, "her cheeks were rouged and her lips appeared pendulous under think layers of lipstick." She spoke about her background largely in narrative fashion, frequently describing her upbringing and key events from her life in an uninterrupted monologue.

According to her testimony, Martha Jule Seabrook was born on May 6, 1920 in Milton, one of the oldest cities in Florida located by the Blackwater River in the western panhandle of the state. The brown-eyed girl with matching brown hair was the youngest of five children. She had three older sisters and a brother, but twenty years separated Martha from her oldest sister, Vera, who had been born during her mother's previous marriage. Her mother, Julia Seabrook, was 44 when Martha was born, a remarkably old age to carry a child to term at the time.

Martha's father, Holland Stanley Seabrook, established the *Santa Rosa Clarion*, which was one of the first weekly newspapers in the area when he started it in 1907. He later served as a printer for its successor, the *Milton Gazette*, where he worked for over twenty years. Though a successful newspaperman, Stanley "never wore the pants in his own home." Instead, there was "constant conflict" between Martha's mother and father. They slept in separate bedrooms and to the young Martha it seemed like there was never a time when they were not arguing.

Affectionately called "Baby" by her father, Martha was an obedient, well-behaved daughter during her childhood. Often shy and quiet around others, Martha grew to resent her mother's favoritism toward her oldest sister, pointing out that she "always placed Vera on a pedestal before me." By the time Martha was nine, a glandular disorder caused her to physically mature much earlier than most girls. At a young age, she developed wide hips, large, prominent breasts, and she began menstruating. Boys and men began noticing her, even male members of her own family. She recalled one incident in which a visiting uncle molested her by feeling her breasts and telling her that he would give her money if she would "play with his penis." Martha's parents separated soon afterward, but her father remained in Milton and continued to see the children, albeit only occasionally.

In August 1933 when she was just thirteen, Martha's seventeen-year-old brother, Dudley, "pushed his attentions" on her and "forced [her] to have relationship with him." While their mother and sisters were at the movies, Dudley raped Martha on the playroom floor on the second-story of the family home. As he caressed and fondled her, Dudley told his barely teenaged sister that he had "learned a new game that he and other boys had been playing and he wanted to teach it to me." When she tried to resist, he pinned her to the ground. When his penis penetrated her, she "suffered considerable pain" and it made her bleed. Afterward, he told her that "it would be best not to tell my mother about it; that she wouldn't understand." Ten days later, he raped her again. This time it hurt even more. When she begged him to stop, "he told me to shut my mouth or he would kill me."

Martha's personality changed after the rapes. She became easily frightened and inherently shy. Her mother became suspicious two months later when she noticed Martha felt sick in the mornings and had missed two menstrual periods. Following stern questioning from her mother, Martha admitted that she had "let a boy get on top" of her, and after further prodding she identified her brother as that boy.

Instead of comforting or supporting her, Martha's mother reacted with anger and accused her of lying, until Dudley finally admitted it. Even then, Martha took the brunt of her mother's fury. Julia bemoaned the fact that her daughter was such a bad apple that had caused the family to lose its self-respect and the respect of the community. She made Martha swallow turpentine and sugar to abort the pregnancy, and when that did not work, she "went down to what we in the South call Nigger Town and talked to an old colored mammy there and she came back and she fixed up a preparation for me." It was a mixture of gunpowder, sugar, and sweet milk that Julia gave Martha to drink. That toxic cocktail was more effective: Martha started menstruating again the day after drinking it.

Having taken care of the incestuous pregnancy, Julia instituted a strict policy of control over Martha. The stringent rules and nearly constant surveillance by Julia did not go unnoticed by Martha's class-mates, who began calling her Martha's "watch dog." Julia also warned her daughter what would happen if she "let a boy get on top" of her again: "she told me that I had gotten off very lightly that time; that if I ever attempted or if she ever found out anything like that took place again that there were places where bad girls could be locked up and that she would see that I was locked up in one of those places."

When it came time for Senior Prom, Martha was only allowed to go if her brother came along as an escort, a condition which was of course highly "embarrassing and uncomfortable" for Martha and her date. Her mother's strict limitations and oppressive control gave Martha a permanent self-image as the "black sheep" of the family. Yet, even with the stifling presence of her overbearing mother, Martha remained an exemplary student with excellent school attendance. In addition to earning good grades, she served as assistant editor of her high school paper, wrote plays as part of the school theater program, played volleyball and basketball, and held an officer's position in the women's club.

While staying with relatives one summer in Monroeville, Alabama, Martha befriended a 12-year-old boy. The boy took such a liking to the "older woman" that he decided to run away with her and the two hitch-hiked their way to Evergreen, a town about thirty miles away. They stayed in a hotel run by Martha's uncle until a hotel clerk reported them and they were returned to their parents. Martha's young suitor that summer of 1936 was Truman Capote, who would go on to write the seminal true crime novel, *In Cold Blood*.

At age eighteen, Martha graduated from Milton High School in 1938, ranked seventh in her class. The graduation class yearbook prophecy of the "quiet" and "shy' student predicted that "[s]he will be a nurse and help the ill to regain their health." After graduation, she took a job as librarian for the Women's Club, where she read vora-ciously. Escaping into the works of writers such as Shakespeare, Alexander Dumas, Alfred Tennyson, and Walter Scott, she began daydreaming about living a life like the dynamic characters in the books she read. Her real life offered nothing as uplifting and exciting as what she found in the pages of those romantic tales. Many nights she thought about how happy the women in the stories seemed to be, and Martha wondered whether she would ever experience that kind of happiness in her own life.

> When I read a novel that was very interesting, or that the heroine was going through a very romantic period, I would dream and plan and wonder how it would be if that was in real life and it had happened to me rather than just being fiction...When I would go to bed at night, rather than being able to relax and go to sleep, I would consider thinking back over how happy the different women in the stories were, and I used to wonder if I would ever be able to have such happiness.

Q. And were you dreaming constantly of being in love?

A. I would say that I was, yes.

Q. And being loved by someone?

A. That is true.

Enlightened with a barometer against which she could compare her own life, Martha vowed that when she started her own family it would be "entirely different" from the family life she had known growing up.

While working for the Women's Club, she caught the eye of a young man who started coming in every day and asking her to have lunch with him. She resisted his advances at first, but eventually agreed to go to the movies with him. When her mother found out she forbid Martha from going and though she pretended to obey, in reality Martha refused to cancel the date. When the night of the date arrived, Martha's mother noticed her getting dressed to go out.

"What are you getting all spruced up for?" her mother asked, her raised eyebrows conveying disbelief and alarm.

"I told you several days ago that I have a date tonight," Martha replied nonchalantly as she continued getting ready.

"Well, I told you to break it."

Martha turned to face Julia with a look of exasperation readily discernible on her face.

"Mother, you have been living my life long enough. It's time for me to start living for myself."

"You don't know how to live your life," her mother replied in an astonished and condescending tone.

Martha glared at her with the furious eyes of an enraged bull about to charge.

"If you don't stop talking to me like that, like I'm always some little child, you're going to drive me crazy!" Martha screamed bitterly.

"I'm going to drive you crazy? You've been crazy all your life!" her mother sneered.

Before Martha could respond, a knock at the door announced the arrival of her date. Without another word or so much as a backward glance, she grabbed her coat and walked out the door. But she could not escape from her mother's influence so easily. Less than a half hour after settling into her seat at the movie theater, Martha heard loud coughing behind her. When she turned around, she was mortified to see her mother sitting in the very next row. Embarrassed, angry, and upset, Martha insisted that her date take her home and then she rushed out of the theater.

After the humiliation of her mother following her when she tried to go on an ordinary date, Martha decided that the only way she would ever have a chance to live a normal life would be to move out on her own. In order to do that she needed to find a job, and she already had something in mind.

A few weeks earlier, two female friends of hers had died. There were only two funeral homes in Milton and when Martha went to the funeral service for her friends she noticed that all of the caretakers were men. She wondered why women who died had to be taken care of by men, and the more she thought about it, the more she came to resent it.

"I felt at the time that if I became an embalmer that perhaps even though the person were dead, I might be able to give a little ease to the loved ones by knowing that a woman was taking care of their female loved ones," she later explained.

However, her sisters soon talked her out of becoming a mortician, convincing her to instead pursue nursing as a profession, where she could "do just as much good." To that end, Martha's oldest sister, Vera, drove her from Milton to Pensacola so she should inquire about nursing school, but it appeared that a nursing career was not yet in the cards. The Mother Superior in charge of the hospital's nursing program informed her that the current class was already full and she would have to wait six or eight months to apply for the next class. Discouraged, Martha accompanied her sister as she ran some errands downtown. While there they bumped into their family doctor, Richard Spencer, who asked what they were doing in Pensacola. The obviously disappointed Martha explained how she had hoped to begin nursing school, but now had to wait over half a year to apply for a spot in the next class. Doctor Spencer considered Martha's story for a moment.

"Do you really want to be a nurse?" he asked.

"Yes, sir, I really, really do," she replied with an earnest smile.

"Do you think you'd be a good nurse?"

"I would certainly try to be."

"Alright, I'll tell you what," Dr. Spencer grinned, "why don't you come over to my office and I'll see what I can do."

Eager to accept whatever help he could provide, Martha followed Spencer to his Pensacola office and watched curiously as he picked up the phone. After being connected to the hospital, he asked to speak to the Mother Superior in charge of the nursing program.

"This is Dr. Spencer," he said when the Mother Superior got on the line. "I have Martha Jule Seabrook here in my office, and she informs me that she wants to be a nurse."

"Yes, I saw her earlier today," the Mother Superior replied. "Unfortunately, the current class is full and there aren't any openings."

"Forget your quota," Spencer quipped, politely admonishing the nun. "Find room for one more. She will make a dandy nurse."

Martha was so excited that she nearly kissed Dr. Spencer, but gave him a grateful hug instead. Then she drove back to the hospital where a nursing supervisor was waiting for her. She was given an application to the Pensacola School of Nursing and told that she could join the current class that would be starting in two weeks.

In her application, Martha wrote:

I chose this profession, for, in this field of endeavor I sincerely believe that I can do my best in aiding humanity. I chose this profession without thought of self and want to prepare myself for this profession, not for material gains but for the purpose of aiding humanity and rendering services to others.

When she started her nursing training, Martha pledged to herself that she "would treat every patient; white, colored, rich or poor, the same, and that I would give him the treatment that I would expect a nurse to render to me or my family in case they came into the hospital."

By the time she began nursing school, Martha had fully grown into her 5'8" heavy-set frame. A "fleshy woman with a ready laugh," she weighed around 180 pounds and had an "awkward body" with "boxer-like shoulders," but "unusually thin legs" and "small, immaculate feet" to go along with a "gentle" voice, "soft" eyes, and a "sweet" face.

Her supervisor at Sacred Heart Hospital wrote that she was a *good nurse in theory and practice. She demonstrated marked executive ability and a pleasing personality.* Similarly, a doctor there wrote in a recommendation: *Her character has proven good all through training. We feel here that she is very efficient.*

In March 1942, Martha graduated and took the state nurse's exam, earning the highest grade average in her class on her way to becoming a registered nurse. Confident from her high marks, she began applying for open positions and landed interview after interview. Despite her impressive scores, virtually every nurse in Martha's class obtained a job before her. It quickly became clear that potential employers were passing her over after seeing her large physical stature.

Martha had to move across the country to get a nursing job, finding one at last when she took a position in July as an operating room nurse at Vallejo General Hospital in Vallejo, California. Despite her nontraditional physical appearance, Martha proved herself to be a valuable nurse. Supervisors found her to be "neat, normal, and interesting...friendly, but not forward," and a co-worker described her as "talkative, brilliant, and punctual." However, the new job and location did nothing to alleviate her loneliness. She began spending much of her free time hanging around bus stations and railroad depots, flirting with the soldiers and sailors arriving on a revolving basis for a few days leave. Three months later, Martha accepted an offer to work as a nurse at a private medical practice, but her bad luck with men continued.

A one-night stand with a Vallejo bus driver left her pregnant, and then, less than two weeks after starting her new job, she was fired after slapping a doctor who fondled her in his office. On her way out of the medical practice, she passed by a medicine cabinet. The one-two punch of the pregnancy and firing was too much for Martha to bear. Something in her snapped. Making sure no one could see her, she opened the medicine cabinet, poured out a handful of sleeping tablets, and stuffed them in her coat pocket. As she walked home, she decided what she would do: "I had in mind that, if I went home and I had to take one more argument from my mother, that life wasn't worth living, if each and every day I had to be nagged continually, and I would rather be dead than to continue living a life like that. I was going to commit suicide."

When Martha told her mother what had happened, she "threw it up in my face that every time I came in contact with a man something like that happened. So that is when I turned around and I left the room and I went into the bathroom and I took the sleeping pills." She swallowed about fourteen pills in all, then wrote a short letter to an ambulance driver who had befriended her: "I explained to him that I thought the best thing for me and for my family, since they looked upon me as being a black sheep, the best thing for me to do would be to end it all." With the letter in hand, she walked to a mailbox about a half-block from her house, growing dizzier and dizzier along the way. She dropped the envelope into the slit and felt so weak that she had to steady herself by holding onto the mailbox.

The next thing she knew, Martha woke up in the psychiatric ward of Mission Emergency Hospital in San Francisco, about 35 miles from Vallejo. Suffering from amnesia, she could not remember how she had ended up there. An intern informed her that she had shown up at a police station in San Francisco in a taxi, telling police that she had become confused and did not know who she was or anything that had happened prior to that morning. After that she was taken to the hospital. A psychiatrist on staff found that she *was not oriented to her own person and remote memory was extinct except for hazy recollection.* He diagnosed her with *hysteria, amnesic type.* Three days later, her memory returned as mysteriously as it had left, and she was released.

Still distraught about her unplanned pregnancy, Martha moved back to Pensacola. Wearing a diamond engagement ring and a wedding band, she announced that she had married Joseph Edward Carmen, a Navy officer, who she met while in California. She described him as being six feet tall with wavy blond hair, "sensitive features," and "blue eyes that crinkled when he smiled." Since the ceremony had taken place in the Naval Chapel in Norfolk, Virginia, and Joseph Carmen was on active duty during a time of war, Martha's friends and family understood that they could not meet him. They were satisfied to simply offer their congratulations to Martha on landing such a catch.

The story worked for a while. It allowed Martha to deliver her first child free from the stigma of giving birth outside the bonds of marriage. But she knew that at some point people would wonder why Carmen never took leave to come see his baby. Martha decided that she could not maintain the ruse indefinitely. One morning, she appeared at the hospital weeping and nearly hysterical. To put an end to the charade, Martha told her fellow nurses that she had received a telegram from the Navy informing her that her husband had been "killed in action in the battle of the Pacific."

In January 1944, Martha started a new job as superintendent of Pensacola Maternity Hospital. Two months later, she became pregnant following another one-night stand. Though she was tempted to get an abortion, Martha decided she wanted to have the baby. "I thought: Perhaps if I can have the baby I can have something of my own to love and that I could forget my past life and be a fit mother."

On May 31, Martha resigned from her position at the hospital so she could prepare for the birth of her illegitimate child. Less than a month later, Martha met bus driver Alfred Willard Beck. They became romantically involved despite the fact that Martha was six months pregnant at the time. On September 26, 1944, Martha gave birth to her daughter, Willadean Carmen, named after Joseph Carmen even though he was not the child's father.

Three months later, on the morning of December 13, Martha married Alfred Beck at the Escambia County Courthouse in Pensacola. That same day, they moved into a house that Alfred had recently rented. They had barely begun their new life together when, at 5:30 p.m. that evening, someone knocked on the front door. Martha answered the door to find a woman with four children standing there.

"You've taken my husband away from me," the woman said with a spiteful stare. "Since you took my man, you get to take his children too!"

With that, the woman turned around and walked away, leaving the children on the steps.

Martha stood there in shock before collecting herself and calling for her new husband. It was a bizarre start to what Martha hoped would be a good marriage. Somehow, they worked their way through it, and by March Martha was pregnant with Beck's child. However, the marriage began to fall apart. After contracting gonorrhea and learning that Beck was having an affair, Martha filed for divorce in May 1945. Seven months later, she gave birth to their son, Anthony.

In February 1946, Martha accepted a position in Pensacola as general staff nurse with the Northwest Florida Crippled Children's Home, a group home established by the American Legion to care for young polio victims. She excelled in her new position and after six months, the home's Board of Directors unanimously approved her promotion to Superintendent overseeing nine nurses, a physiotherapist, two cooks, and three maids. However, the new responsibilities only temporarily relieved her loneliness, and she turned to drinking to dull her aching heart. Longing for true romance, she easily fell for her friend Elizabeth Swanson's fateful joke of joining a lonely hearts club.

"If it hadn't been for that joke, I wouldn't be in the courtroom now," she told the jury in an earnest tone.

Though it had been a friendly act with good intentions behind it, submitting Martha's name to the club brought dire consequences, sweeping her up in a vortex of emotion that soon led her permanently astray.

Chapter Twenty-Two

Having given the jury a detailed look at Martha's background of sexual abuse, mental problems, and trouble with men, Rosenberg shifted his inquiry to another area he hoped would help strengthen the insanity defense: her sexual relationship with Ray. It would also help answer the question lodged in the minds of the jurors: why would a well-educated woman with a good job who had never before broken the law lose her way and turn to crime? What could cause her to suddenly become a cold-blooded murderer?

Martha was not the least bit bashful about her "abnormal sexual relations" with Ray. She testified in detail regarding their use of fellatio and cunnilingus, which a doctor had recommended so that she could be sexually satisfied.

"He told me that often those measures would bring forth satisfaction when the average normal intercourse would not," Martha explained to the transfixed jury, "and he told me not to look upon those as being something ugly or vulgar; that when two people loved each other, that no matter what they did, it was not to be considered abnormal."

The doctor asked her whether "at any time in early childhood, if I had had any affair or anything that would prevent me from enjoying a relationship, and I had told him about the incident with my brother, and he told me that he imagined that that was the root of the case."

Rosenberg felt that Martha's enthusiastic participation in fellatio and cunnilingus, her unembarrassed willingness to talk about it in open court, and the fact that she saw nothing wrong with the behavior would cast her as deviant and psychologically abnormal in the eyes of the jury. This would, he believed, predispose them to finding her insane.

"The lovemaking between the defendant Fernandez and I, that you have described as being abnormal, is something that took place because we loved each other," she told the jurors with a sincere expression, "and I consider that something practically sacred."

"You do not consider it abnormal?" Rosenberg asked.

"For the love that I had for Mr. Fernandez, nothing we did was abnormal," she proclaimed.

After each "abnormal" lovemaking session, Martha "would be in practically an unconscious condition or motionless," and she confirmed that Ray was "the first and the only" man who ever enabled her to enjoy sex.

"I became emotionally aroused every time I was in touching distance of Mr. Fernandez," she said.

Martha also explained a term of endearment, "Oscar," which she used for a part of Ray's body.

"Each year in the spring an academy award is presented in Hollywood to the best performer and the best supporting role," Martha explained with a wry smile. "In my estimation Mr. Fernandez was the best performer in my private life and the part of his body with the best supporting role, which was his penis, I named Oscar."

To drive home the extent of her sexual addiction to Ray, Rosenberg asked Martha why she had helped cover up Janet Fay's murder, including preparing several letters to banks falsifying information about Janet Fay's finances. Martha did not skip a beat.

"Because a request from Mr. Fernandez to me was a command," she said simply. "I love him enough that I would have done anything that he asked me to do. If, in the end, he and I would be married, I would have consented to anything."

Love was a vicious motivator for Martha's actions, and the psychological influence Ray wielded over her became the underlying theme of her defense at trial. During their relationship, Ray's power over Martha, the extent of his authority over her actions, had become an instance of life imitating art. Like Charles Boyer's character in *Gaslight*, Ray's mistreatment of her – his systematic pursuit of other women with callous disregard of Martha's feelings – constituted an insidious form of abuse that caused her spiral into insanity.

Returning to the narrative that Martha blacked out and was not conscious of her acts at the time of Janet Fay's murder, Rosenberg repeated his questions from several days earlier in the trial about her memory of the event.

Q: Did you strike Janet J. Fay twice on the head with a hammer?

A: I have no recollection of striking Janet J. Fay at all.

Q. Did you ever plan with the defendant Fernandez to strike Janet J. Fay on the head with a hammer?

A. No, sir.

The bludgeoning of Janet Fay had been a sudden act of blind fury, ignited by an intense jealousy, itself spawned by a deep-seeded fear of abandonment tracing back to Martha's history of dysfunctional relationships. That cycle of failed relationships was a primal wound that never went away. The festering loneliness and pain built to a boiling point and then erupted all at once in a savage, berserk attack.

Martha's testimony at trial about the murder mirrored that of Ray's in contending that Martha had been in some sort of daze when Ray came out of the bathroom and saw her standing over Janet's body. It was like waking from a hazy dream. She only regained her senses when Ray shook her shoulders and asked what she had done. She followed Ray's eyes to Janet's bloodied body on the floor. The nurse in her sprang into action, kneeling down to see if Janet had a pulse, but it was too late.

Whether by mistake or strategic design, Martha's testimony at trial muddied the waters with respect to what actually happened during the moments leading up to Janet's murder. Testimony that contradicted her or Ray's prior statements included the whereabouts and circumstances of the murder instrument: the hammer that fractured Janet's skull.

Q. Do you recall at any time the defendant Fernandez going downstairs to get a hammer?

A. No, sir.

Q. Do you recall him at any time putting a hammer on the icebox?

A. No, sir.

Q. And do you recall him at any time telling you that he might have to use that hammer during the night?

A. No, sir.

Q. Did the defendant Fernandez at any time say to you, "Keep that woman quiet. I don't care how you do it"?

A. No, sir.

Martha also claimed that just before she spoke to Edward Robinson for the first time while still being held in Michigan, Clarence Randle approached her and warned her about questions pertaining to the murder weapon.

"He said: 'Now, Martha, for God's sake, don't tell anybody I told you this or I'll lose my job but [Robinson] has brought in some tools and among them he has several hammers he is going to try to have you identify. But be careful what you say, and no matter what he asks you, say you have never seen the hammers before.'"

That was why she did not identify the murder weapon and instead said that she "didn't recall having seen it or it didn't look like the one or it was too large, it was too small. I was remembering what Randle had told me to say." That was, she now claimed, also the reason why her supplemental statement given March 11 had asserted that Ray did retrieve the hammer from his car and indicated the need to use it on Janet shortly before her murder.

Rosenberg made sure to portray Randle's alleged hammer advice as part of the reason for inconsistencies between his clients' statements in Michigan and their testimony at trial, which they now claimed to be the true narrative of Janet Fay's murder.

Q. At any time while you were in the State of Michigan were you concerned with the truthfulness of your answers?

A. No, sir, and if I am not mistaken I told more lies than the truth.

....

Q. Did you tell [Attorney Verspoor] anything concerning the truth of these statements?

A. I told him that what they wanted me to say, that there was no truth in it whatsoever. He says, "You mean that you are going to give them another statement which will contain more lies?" And I said, "Yes, sir."

"They tortured me in mind so much that night, telling me different things about Ray, breaking my faith, trying to make me lose confidence in him, that by the next day I was willing to tell them anything that they wanted me to," Martha explained. "Because Clarence Randle and Sheriff Blacklock had tortured my mind so that I was willing to tell anything that they told me to say, and the statement that was given that day is practically a word-for-word conversation that Blacklock and Randle prepared for me to say."

Martha's trial testimony also continued to shift the responsibility for Janet's murder away from Ray, keeping the timing of his participation limited to events that occurred after Janet's death.

Q. Was the deceased Janet J. Fay at any time moaning and groaning in the presence of the defendant Fernandez?

A. No, sir.

Q. Did the defendant Fernandez put a scarf around the neck of the deceased Janet J. Fay?

A. Around the deceased; yes, sir.

Q. Was she alive or dead at that time.

A. Dead.

Q. Is there any question in your mind about it?

A. None whatsoever.

Q. Was there any blood on the floor at that time?

A. Yes, sir.

Q. How much blood, if you know?

A. There was a very large amount of blood.

Q. Enough to cause the death of Janet J. Fay?

A. Very easily, yes.

There was so much blood that it saturated her and Ray's clothes as they tried to clean up the crime scene. Martha recalled blood being "all over the rug and my housecoat, my gown, Mr. Fernandez's pajamas, and on the gown and robe that Mrs. Fay had on."

Rosenberg steered his direct examination of Martha to belabor the fact that Janet was not alive when Ray twisted the scarf around her neck like a tourniquet. He asked Martha whether she had been concerned at the time that the scarf might harm Janet.

"The woman was already dead," Martha said confidently. "My only intentions were to stop the blood from getting all over the floor. I couldn't very well cause the death of a person already dead."

Continuing his direct examination of Martha on the morning of July 29, Rosenberg caused a stir by requesting a reenactment of Janet Fay's murder, a request that drew a stern rejection by Judge Pecora.

Mr. Rosenberg: Would you be willing, Mrs. Beck to, if the Court approved it, to submit to an actual reenactment of the scene of the alleged crime?

Mr. Robinson: Objection.

The Court: Objection sustained. It is not possible to reproduce it.

Mr. Rosenberg: I was going to make an application to your Honor, after the witness indicated whether she was willing. May I at this time request your Honor – I know the application is new, it is novel and unique, and it may be that we [are] pioneering in the field of criminology.

The Court: I see no occasion for any such pioneering venture under the facts of this case.

Mr. Rosenberg: Up to the present time, if your Honor please, we only have a word picture of what has taken place.

The Court: Up to the present time this witness has testified that her mind was virtually a blank at a certain period of time that it seems to me is a vital period of time. How can she hope to reproduce it?

After Rosenberg completed his direct examination, the totality of Martha's testimony suggested an overall defense strategy of limiting Ray's involvement in Janet's death to that of an accessory after-the-fact, while minimizing Martha's legal responsibility by insulating her culpability for premeditated murder under circumstances of legal insanity. However, on cross examination, the lead prosecutor challenged Martha's story that Janet Fay slapped her and the next thing she knew Janet was slouched over bleeding on the floor.

"As she slapped you, then, you blacked out like this?" Assistant State Attorney Edward Robinson asked, snapping his fingers to emphasize his disbelief.

"Yes," Martha replied, eyeing him like a serpent ready to strike.

Before, during, and after her testimony, she showed irritation about Judge Pecora's frequent rulings against the defense on evidentiary matters. When Rosenberg attempted to ask her about the Governor's agreement that resulted in Ray and Martha being extradited to New York, the judge again ruled that he could not pursue further questions about the agreement. But the ruling did not deter her.

"It's a cinch if it weren't for that agreement we wouldn't be here today," Martha snapped.

"Please, Mrs. Beck," the judge cautioned her, "just confine yourself to answering questions. Don't tell me what I should do."

"I don't know whether you remember it or not, but this is my life that is at stake, and not yours," Martha shot back, staring at him as if she could see into his very soul.

Chapter Twenty-Three

On August 2, Herbert Rosenberg surprised nearly everyone in the courtroom by announcing that the defense was withdrawing the insanity plea with respect to Ray. The defense would still be raised on behalf of Martha, but Ray's scowling face after Rosenberg's announcement expressed his exasperation with the legal strategy to abandon it for his case.

"I'm not the guy who needs a psychiatrist," he told reporters afterward.

Rosenberg followed up the plea withdrawal with what the *Daily News* called "probably the longest question ever asked in any court." Over a two-day period he took over 5 hours, 40,000 words, and 250 pages worth of trial transcript to properly phrase his question to psychiatrist Richard Hoffmann about Martha's mental state at the time of the crime.

Known for treating high-profile patients such as *The Great Gatsby* author F. Scott Fitzgerald, Dr. Hoffmann served as the defense's chief medical expert at trial. During Rosenberg's extensive questioning, Hoffmann opined that Martha was "laboring under such a defect of reason as not to know that the act was wrong." But on cross examination by the prosecution, Dr. Hoffmann acknowledged that his opinion "relied entirely upon the truth of her statements," including that she had momentarily blacked out after being slapped by Janet Fay.

Upon further questioning during cross, Hoffmann elaborated on the grounds of his opinion with regard to Martha's alleged "compulsive, tensive irresistible obsession or act."

Q. Is it your opinion that she thought or knew that the act was a proper act, was a right act, as distinguished from a wrong one?

A. No, I think she can tell right and wrong and knows that difference, but at that time she could no more control her conduct than she could have controlled an asthmatic attack.

Q. Then what you mean, Doctor, is that this was some irresistible impulse?

A. Yes, sir.

Q. You do not mean then that she didn't know it was wrong?

A. She didn't know it was wrong if it was an irresistible impulse, because you haven't the time to think whether it is right or wrong at that time.

.....

Q. How long did the defendant Mrs. Beck suffer from a defect of reason which did not enable her to know that the act was wrong?

A. It lasted as long as a blind fury can last. This is what we call a succession of impulses...there comes a time when the straw breaks the camel's back, and in that moment when you lose your temper, and you do that which is nearest to you, in order to escape from the demon within you, you cannot know right from wrong, or you wouldn't have done it.

In Dr. Hoffmann's opinion, Martha was in such a state of "blind fury" that she could not stop to think about whether the act of striking Janet on the head with a hammer was right or wrong. Simply put, the "demon within" lashed out without Martha having any control over it.

Of course, the prosecution's chief psychiatric expert, Dr. Perry Lichenstein, disagreed with Hoffmann's assessment of Martha's state of mind. According to Lichenstein, Martha knew the "nature and quality of the act and that the act was wrong" and that the hammer was a "dangerous weapon" capable of causing fatal injuries to Janet Fay. He disputed the defense's contention that Martha went into an amnesiac state or blacked out immediately prior to and during her attack on Janet. He conceded that someone in a true amnesiac state would not know what they were doing was wrong and therefore could not be legally responsible for their actions. However, Lichenstein clarified that Martha would not have been able to snap out of such an amnesiac state and have the presence of mind to check Janet's pulse, contrary to what she testified she did immediately after Ray shook her. Instead, Martha would have gradually regained awareness as the black-out condition tapered off.

Q. Doctor, from your examination of the defendant...can you state with reasonable certainty whether or not in your opinion the defendant Martha Beck at the time of the killing of Mrs. Fay had any amnesia?

A. In my opinion she did not.

Q. Will you give us your reasons for that, Doctor?

A. It is my opinion that it would be impossible for this woman to have an amnesia and not recall at any time before the act or after the act, even if we exclude during the act, that she ever had some hammer, that she had some weapon, that she struck her. Another thing is when Fernandez came to her and put his hands on her and shook her, she immediately came out of the amnesia; she was able to go down on her knees or bend down and feel the pulse...an amnesia does not end that way. It doesn't.

Q. How does it end, Doctor?

A. There is usually a gradual tapering off and the person has an emotional disturbance after it. He is not very, very calm...Another thing is they usually do not go for any spot which is known as a deadly area, a lethal area. They hit in every direction because the person is not fully conscious. They do not go for one particular place. And in this case the two wounds were in the skull, a vital spot.

During Rosenberg's cross examination of Lichenstein, the doctor admitted that it would be possible for a person to know the nature and quality of an act and yet not know that the act is wrong "if there is a definite mental condition there preceding it." But based on his examination of Martha, he felt confident in concluding that she had no such preceding mental condition. Lichenstein acknowledged that Martha would not be legally responsible for Janet Fay's murder if she had experienced a true amnesia during the attack, but stuck to his opinion that she did not have an amnesia event.

After rehashing Martha's suicide attempts and sexual experiences, Rosenberg asked Lichenstein if such events should be taken into account when assessing her psychological state at the time of the killing. Lichenstein paused and his eyes narrowed slightly as he considered the question.

"Interesting," he finally replied, "but not important." Regardless of the traumatic events she may have experienced in the past, he maintained that Martha knew what she was doing when she killed Janet Fay.

The prosecution's other expert, Dr. James McCartney, agreed with Lichenstein that Martha did not have a true episode of amnesia because after such an episode there would be a "period of confusion" and there could not be an immediate "resumption of all full faculties" such as Martha described after twice striking Janet with the hammer. In his opinion, Martha "at all times knew what she was doing; she knew the nature and quality of her act, and she knew that it was wrong."

McCartney acknowledged that there were relevant parts of Martha's background that should be assessed to determine whether she qualified as a psychopathic personality knowing the difference between right and wrong, but not "wanting to adhere to the rules of right and wrong," and choosing instead to "purposefully indulge [her] own whims."

Rosenberg asked about various events from Martha's background, including her apparent dependence on Ray, but McCartney ultimately declined to categorize Martha as a psychopathic personality.

Q. Would you consider it important to know that the defendant Beck was so attracted to a man like the defendant Fernandez that she couldn't leave him out of her sight?

A. Oh, it would be considered and yet there are lots of women who will take lots of abuse and they still hang onto their husbands.

Frances Sobel, another psychiatrist retained by Rosenberg who had administered a Rorschach Test to Martha during trial preparation, was prevented by the court from testifying about her "psychopathic character." After hearing all of the expert testimony pertaining to Martha's insanity defense, Judge Pecora expressed doubts as to whether it had been properly invoked.

"The trouble is I think you are trying to ride two horses that are going in different directions at the same time," the judge told Rosenberg. "She avoids admitting the act and then she says, 'But having done the act, I am to be legally excused because of my state of mind at the time.'"

Martha could only hope that the jury did not share Judge Pecora's opinion.

Chapter Twenty-Four

A t 10:30 on the morning of August 15, Rosenberg stood up from the defense table and began his closing argument to the jury. Anyone hoping for a concise articulation of the defense's case would be sorely disappointed. Rather than a succinct framing of the case, Ray and Martha's attorney took over six and a half hours to complete his closing. Stranger still, he freely admitted that his clients were guilty of a serious criminal offense.

After referring to the "dark shadows of this frightful crime," Rosenberg looked each juror in the eye and told them:

> I talk from my heart. I am going to plead just as if the defendants were part of me. But the only thing I am going to plead here is for their life. I am not concerned with their liberty. I am concerned with their life. They are charged with a crime here punishable by death in the electric chair, and the only reason I stand here is to see that they do not go to the electric chair.

Evoking the *foile a deux* defense, he called the case "pathetic – a tragedy besides the actual killing. The tragedy is how these two defendants or why these two defendants should ever have met." Rosenberg's words sought to cast Ray and Martha as hapless victims swept along by forces beyond their control, pawns of cruel Fate. He explained Ray's failure to report Martha's killing of Janet Fay to police as something he could not help "because they were so involved sexually that it was impossible for them to act as normal persons."

Then he delivered a new thrust of his defense strategy:

> There were times during this trial when I just felt like a little boy down along the ocean front playing around with shells and pebbles, with the whole ocean of undiscovered truth ahead of me. I felt like that on numerous occasions until one day I discovered what in my opinion is the truth of this case, the whole truth, and nothing but the truth.

That truth centered on the physical evidence of Janet Fay's murder. Reminding the jury about the prosecution's allegation that Janet was leaning over her suitcase with her back to Martha when Martha hit her with the hammer, Rosenberg reiterated the medical examiner's testimony that the hammer blows caused injuries to the right side of Janet's head. Then he came to the Perry Mason moment of his closing statement, the part that he believed would win the jury over on the issue of Martha's innocence of first-degree murder.

> Mrs. Beck happens to be lefthanded. Bear that in mind, folks. She is lefthanded. Now, take Mrs. Beck, lefthanded, with the hammer. Let me walk over to Mrs. Fay who is bending down with her back to her, and show me how Mrs. Beck could have struck her on the right side of the head. It is a physical impossibility.

> Now, I say that in and of itself should create a reasonable doubt, and if you do not find the defendant Beck or the defendants here guilty beyond a reasonable doubt, you must acquit them of the crime of murder in the first degree.

Rosenberg completed his closing argument the next day. Although he represented both defendants, his closing continued to focus on why Martha should not be deemed responsible for the crime, portraying her as having been controlled by an overwhelming passion that she could not resist.

> Now, love is a very peculiar thing to a woman. Love is just an episode in a man's life, but it is the very life of a woman. A woman lives for love and a man does not. And Mrs. Beck became so wrapped up in the defendant Fernandez that she was just like another hand to him. That is what love did and is still doing to the defendant Beck.

> And nobody can say why one person feels that way towards another, or nobody can account why a man has a certain love for a maid, or why a king marries a commoner. Poets and everybody else have tried to write about this from the beginning of history, and they are still continuing. That is love. And there is no question about it in my mind, that it is an indescribable love that Martha Beck has for the defendant Fernandez. And passion can overthrow reason.

Martha's love for Ray ran so deep, its pull grew so powerful, that she could not be expected to act in any other way than she did. If anything, Rosenberg argued, Martha's only crime was loving the wrong man. That love begot a dangerous jealousy which short-circuited rational thinking and overcame all sense of morality, culminating in the tragedy of Janet Fay's death.

> Mrs. Beck's brain was twisted on the early morning hour of January 4th...and that twisted brain started going into a frenzy....She was fearful of losing the one person in her life that meant more than even her own children, the defendant Fernandez. And when she finally got into this argument with Mrs. Fay...she went into a whirlpool, a blind fury.

Martha and Ray were impressed by Rosenberg's concluding summation. Afterward in the courtroom hallway, they happily clasped

162 • TORTURED WITH LOVE

hands with their bowtie-clad counsel. All three felt optimistic that the
closing had swayed the jury in favor of the defense, but the prosecution's closing argument was still to come.

At 2:00 p.m. on August 16, District Attorney Robinson stood before
the jury to present the state's closing. With the afternoon session of
court about to commence, over 150 people – mostly women – rushed
the doors, pushing and shouting as they realized there were no more
seats inside the courtroom. Right out of the blocks, Robinson shifted
the focus of the case back to the victim.

> We have heard a lot of crying out about the violation of the
> constitutional rights of the defendants. But very little have we heard
> about the right of this poor widow, Janet J. Fay, who lived up in
> Albany, minding her own business, perhaps a little senile, perhaps a
> little silly, but very little have we heard about her right to live. And
> she is not here to tell us about it today.
>
> ....
>
> There is no question about the fact that, without any consideration for
> the right to live of that widow, we find her body tied up as you would
> tie up a bundle of wood, thrown in a hole of a cellar floor in a house
> hired for that purpose by these defendants, dirt filled in on the
> uncovered body, and the floor re-cemented. Janet Fay, as they hoped
> at that time, would be forgotten to the world.

Robinson went on to attack the defendants' credibility and discredit
the version of events they gave in their testimony at trial, urging the
jury to give more weight to what they told investigators during the
initial days after their arrest. He also disputed Rosenberg's contention
that left-handed Martha could not have hit Janet with the hammer
because the blows impacted the right side of Janet's head.

Janet is kneeling over the bag. As she hears her coming, she looks up and it's then that she gets two blows over the head and falls down over the bag. There is no testimony here that the hitting was done from the rear, as counsel would have you believe. No, the body is found right over the bag, where it was. And the blows are right there in the head where she got it from that left-handed woman coming in and giving it to her.

When the State's closing continued at 10:30 the next morning, Robinson focused on Ray and Martha's actions following Janet's murder, including their efforts to cash the checks she had signed shortly before her death. He read to the jury from a fabricated letter dated January 9, 1949, which Martha had presented to one of the banks as having been written by Janet Fay.

Dear Mrs. Beck:

Please find enclosed the signed withdrawal blank that you sent me by Air Mail Special Delivery, after our telephone conversation the other day.

I must tell you how greatly upset and embarrassed I was when you informed me of the difficulty and trouble I had placed upon you, trying to cash my check.

I assure you, had I realized the trouble I was causing, I would never have left New York in such a hurry. I am sure that you will have no further trouble in receiving your money.

I am also sending you my bank pass book. You may send it to the bank with your letter, in case they should wish to have the book to verify the withdrawal of the check or to change the date of the withdrawal.

With the exception of being upset over the trouble I have caused you, I am having a very happy and wonderful time.

Yours truly,
Janet J. Fay

"I am having a very happy and wonderful time," he repeated

sarcastically. "She certainly was," Robinson quipped. "She was in a trunk at that time, dead."

Another fabricated letter he reviewed for the jury was addressed to Ann Mason and dated January 11:

Dear friend Ann:

These few words concern Charles and I, we wish that this letter finds you in a present state of good health. We are both also in a great state of health and are having a wonderful and happy time down here in this tremendous city.

Ann, it is almost silly to say, but I feel as happy and contented as I have ever felt in all my life.

"I guess she did," Robinson interposed. "The poor woman was dead." Then he resumed reading:

I am sorry that I could not go to see you before we left, but you will understand that it was all for the best.

We are planning to go to Florida for the winter, if we like it there we may stay indefinitely there and make our home.

I am so glad that I found someone to love and devote my time to.

Best of wishes and luck to you all.

Love,

Janet J. Fay

Having highlighted how the defendants covered their tracks after the murder, Robinson addressed their attempts to backtrack from the confessions they made shortly after their arrest.

We often wonder, and I have often heard it asked, how does a confession come about? Well, if you think back from your ordinary experience, the human mind can just store up within itself so many wrong things that are done. Sometimes when it gets cornered on one particular wrong thing, it goes overboard, then unloads that thing from the chest. Get it off! Oh, what a relief it is to tell everything, to make a clean breast of everything! Once they start to tell the truth about something, to confess, then they want to confess everything that they have done wrong; get it off; get it over with; make their peace with God.

Trying to deflect part of the defense's strategy of seeking sympathy for the defendants, Robinson recited the harsh events that Ray had testified he had endured, including his physical and mental suffering during the Spanish Civil War. The wily prosecutor wanted to turn Ray's testimony around and paint him as someone easily capable of murder.

"Well, certainly, the things that he has told us about would make one callous to death, absolutely callous," Robinson proclaimed. "Death would mean nothing to him."

Arguing that Ray and Martha's actions had all been deliberate from the very beginning, Robinson wrapped up his closing by redirecting the focus of the case to the forever silenced victim.

This is the crux of the case: Martha Beck and Fernandez joined together in January of 1948 for a definite plan and purpose. They went from one place to another, still together. They admit and tell us that when they went to Albany they had a plan of getting money from Janet Fay. They were determined that that money was going to be in their possession. They were taking no chances, no chances whatsoever that Janet Fay would go out and tell her brother, sister, nephew, or anybody else, that almost $6,000 in cash had gone into the pocket of Fernandez with his concubine Martha Beck.

And then came the death of Janet Fay.

Motive? Filled to the ears with motives. Dead men tell no tales. Janet Fay is dead. A deliberate, premeditated murder.

He paused to let his words linger in the minds of the jurors for a few moments before concluding in the same solemn tone: "I submit the case to you. You have heard their story. You can't hear Janet Fay's."

Chapter Twenty-Five

With both the prosecution and defense having rested their cases, Judge Pecora gave the jury its instructions, recognizing the grueling challenge of the trial being held "through an unusually heated period of the year," which likely contributed to "tempers on the part of either Court or counsel to have gotten frayed here and there." Cognizant of the emotional reaction naturally arising in response to a bloody crime such as the savage bludgeoning murder of Janet Fay, the judge cautioned the jurors not to allow their emotions to dictate guilt or innocence.

> Your duty in this case is simple. You are to say whether or not these defendants, or either of them, are guilty of the crime of homicide in any of the four degrees upon which I have given the case to you for your consideration. Verdicts come from the head, not from the heart. The rendition of a verdict by a jury...is the performance of a duty which involves the use and employment of the faculties of the head, the mind, the brain, not the emotional considerations which spring from the heart.

In other words, the jury should not allow emotions to overcome reasoning, as the defense alleged Martha had done. Judge Pecora's lengthy charge lasted until 11:38 p.m., at which time the jury began its deliberations.

The jury's deliberations continued overnight. Ray's sister, Lena Cano, sat all night in the courtroom with a dozen curious housewives, awaiting the verdict that would decide whether the brother who saved her life in Spain would pay with his own life for his more recent actions in America. Clad in a "dapper" camel hair jacket and tan slacks, Ray waited with Martha in the courthouse holding cell.

Concerned that the jury members might settle on a verdict out of exhaustion simply to end their deliberations, at nearly 2:00 a.m. Rosenberg asked Judge Pecora to allow the jury to retire and continue deliberating after getting some sleep. The judge, eager to end what had been a grueling and lengthy trial, refused. However, several hours later at 5:20 a.m., the court received another request to retire for the night, and this time the request came in writing from the jury itself. After summoning the jury, the judge gave his reply:

> The receipt of this request from you, I assure you, is not surprising to me, and I regret that any necessity has arisen which prompted you to convey this communication to me. It has not thus far been found convenient to comply with it. I realize the possible sense of discomfort that may be caused to you, but until it is found convenient to comply with the request I will ask you to be good enough to continue your deliberations in the case.

> Let us try to suffer a little while longer and please resume your deliberations and then if you deem it necessary to renew the request again I shall be glad to give it consideration.

When the jury left to resume its work, Rosenberg voiced his objection to the court's denial of the request to retire for the night.

"At this time, I think it is putting an undue burden upon the jurors to stay in session any further, especially after that request," he contended, "and I think it may lead them to a hasty decision in this case."

Judge Pecora remained steadfast in insisting that the jury continue deliberating; however, he praised Rosenberg for zealously representing his clients and shook his hand in front of reporters in the courtroom hallway to show there were no hard feelings after their tense confrontations during the trial.

Three hours later, what the judge wanted came to pass. The jury of ten men and two women notified the bailiff that they had reached a verdict, having sat through closing arguments since 10:30 a.m. the day before, the court's lengthy jury charge afterward, and total overnight deliberations of 12 hours and 34 minutes.

Clearly exhausted and "looking haggard" with their clothes noticeably wrinkled from the all-night ordeal of waiting in the courthouse detention pen, Ray and Martha stood stoically at 8:30 a.m. as the jury foreman read the verdict finding them both guilty of first-degree murder. Martha showed no emotion, but gripped the edge of the defense table and glared at Rosenberg after hearing her conviction for first-degree murder.

During the court's polling of the jury Rosenberg noticed that Juror 6, factory employee Samuel Sohmers, hesitated for some time before finally mumbling his assent to the guilty verdict. Rosenberg jotted down the man's name in this trial notebook, determined to pursue the matter at the appropriate time.

After being dismissed by the judge, jurors told reporters that following their first jury ballot, ten voted in favor of first-degree murder for Ray with one voting second degree and one voting manslaughter. For Martha, ten voted for first degree murder, one voted second degree, and one actually voted for acquittal. Rose Hollander, the juror who voted for second degree murder for both defendants soon switched to first degree, while Samuel Sohmers, the juror who originally voted manslaughter for

Ray and acquittal for Martha, held out throughout the night until 3:00 a.m. when he agreed to convict Ray of first-degree murder. Over five hours later, he joined the rest of the jurors by agreeing to convict Martha as well.

After Judge Pecora thanked the jurors for their service and dismissed them, Ray and Martha accompanied Rosenberg to the bar to facilitate preparation for sentencing. Martha's brazen side, which she had shown flashes of during witness testimony and other times during the trial, emerged again when a court administrator asked her name.

"Martha Jule Beck, Martha Jule Carmen, Martha Martin, and Martha Fernandez," she snapped sarcastically.

After leading Martha and Ray back to their seats afterward, Rosenberg squeezed their hands and whispered to them. They both smiled faintly at their attorney while Ray's two sisters wept quietly in the front row of the courtroom gallery.

Afterward, worn down physically and emotionally by the experience, Sohmers shared his thought process with reporters.

"I still think I was right," Sohmers asserted. "Take Fernandez. What proof was there of premeditation? None at all that I can see. And as for Martha, she was crazy when she was born and she still is crazy. Do you send a crazy person to the chair?"

Clearly worn down himself, Edward Robinson admitted that he was "damned surprised" that the jury came back with first-degree murder convictions after such a long deliberation. In his experience, the longer the deliberation, the better the news for the defendant.

As news of the verdict spread, one of the pair's fleecing victims, Esther Henne, told reporters "they got what they deserved." With considerable satisfaction and spite noticeable in her voice, Henne explained that she had been trying to get her marriage to Ray annulled, "but I suppose the electric chair will take care of that matter."

Martin Price, Deliphene Downing's father, similarly praised the jury's verdict, sharing that he felt all along that they deserved the electric chair.

"And the sooner the better as far as I'm concerned," he declared.

At 2:45 on the hot, sticky afternoon of August 22, Ray and Martha appeared for sentencing before Judge Pecora and a packed courtroom of spectators. Martha's demeanor was in sharp contrast to her reaction following the jury verdict when she screamed "I'll kill myself before they put me in that chair!" Neither she nor Ray opted to address the court before imposition of their sentences. Ray stood and showed no emotion as he listened to Judge Pecora sullenly pronounce the sentence of death by electrocution. Martha smiled faintly as the judge's voice briefly broke during his sentencing of her.

In an effort to obtain a new trial, Rosenberg submitted an affidavit that the jury had been "bordering on collapse" in a "state of mental and physical exhaustion" when it reached its verdict.

The silver-haired judge read Rosenberg's affidavit with a pained expression on his face as if he was suffering from a bad case of indigestion.

"I am not in accord with these observations," he said, setting the affidavit aside. "I have conscientious objections to the infliction of capital punishment. That feeling alone would impel me to respect every right of these defendants, but I have a duty to perform."

No matter what personal opinion the judge held about the death penalty, in the eyes of the law the punishment fit the crime. Attempting another approach, Rosenberg argued for over an hour that juror number 6, Samuel Sohmers, had clearly conveyed that he was coerced into joining the first-degree murder verdict, including by various forms of intimidation from other jurors. Rosenberg also asserted that another juror told Sohmers early in the trial: "The defendants should burn – they are guilty as hell." Sohmers had stuck to his convictions as long as he could, but finally, under duress and "against his own good conscience," gave in to the pressure from his fellow jurors as well as his own physical and mental exhaustion.

Rosenberg offered to have Sohmers testify, but the judge refused to hear from him.

"There is a well-established law which says that a juror will not be heard to impeach his own verdict," Judge Pecora declared. "No court should attach any importance to a claim made by a juror, after the verdict has been rendered, that the verdict did not represent his conscientious conclusions. Why, if you could do that," Pecora pointed out, "no verdict would be safe."

Gazing solemnly at the two defendants before him, the judge paused as if struggling to complete the task required of him.

He sentenced Ray first.

> You are hereby sentenced to the punishment of death and it is ordered that within 10 days after this day's session of the court, the Sheriff of the County of the Bronx is to deliver you, Raymond Martinez, to the warden of the State Prison of the State of New York at Sing Sing, where you shall be kept in solitary confinement until the week beginning on Monday, October 10, 1949, and upon some day within the week so appointed the agent and warden of Sing Sing is commanded to do execution upon you in the mode and manner prescribed by the laws of the State of New York.

With nearly identical same words, he sentenced Martha to the same fate. The $5,000 her family paid Herbert Rosenberg to litigate a defense at trial had failed to save either her or her lover. Money fleeced from their many victims had allowed Ray and Martha to live an exuberant lifestyle, but the only currency accepted for their crimes would be their lives.

Chapter Twenty-Six

I mmediately after being sentenced, Ray and Martha were shuttled directly from the Bronx County Courthouse to their new home at Sing Sing Prison. Built in 1825 on the banks of the Hudson River north of New York City, Sing Sing had become the most famous prison in the world, a mythical place that added phrases like "Up the river" and "The Big House" to the American lexicon. "Old Sparky," the first electric chair, had claimed its first victim there in 1891, and for much of the American public, Sing Sing was synonymous with the death penalty. Indeed, more executions had taken place there than at any other American prison.

A rowdy crowd of nearly 100 curious onlookers and paparazzi stood outside the barbed-wire gates of the high-security prison to greet Ray and Martha as they arrived in separate cars. Many shouted insults or shook their fists at the vehicles as they delivered their notorious passengers to the prison's front entrance one at a time. Armed guards in the rounded tower overlooking the entrance watched as Ray and Martha separately climbed the six concrete steps, handcuffed to detectives but "maintaining their usual smiling pose as they walked jauntily through the steel-grilled doors of the prison."

Once inside Sing Sing's "grim, gray" walls, their police escorts transferred custody of the two condemned prisoners to the state prison authorities by handing over Ray and Martha's death warrants and other documentation necessary to complete the transfer. Then prison officials photographed the two newest inmates, forever memorializing their solemn, sullen expressions. Ray's photo in particular conveyed a look of morose bewilderment. Identified as inmate number 108-595, his documentation listed him as just under 5'9", 151 pounds, with the name, "Encarna," tattooed across his heart. Bearing a stoic, resigned expression, Martha – now inmate number 108-594 – measured 5'8 ¾" and weighed in at 202 pounds with prison officials noting a "medium stocky" build on her intake paperwork.

Each of the Lonely Hearts Killers filled out entrance papers that included the question of why they committed the crime for which they had been sentenced. The "Criminal Act Attributed to" section of the Receiving Blotter for Martha reflected the thrust of her defense at trial, recording her response of *Something I got into. I had no control*. Ray similarly disavowed responsibility for his actions, stating: *It was an accident and jealousy on [the] part of two women*.

Having completed the administrative intake process, they boarded a bus to the condemned cell block, the area of the prison that housed convicts awaiting execution. Unlike other prisons, where those awaiting capital punishment did so on "Death Row," the cell area for death-sentence prisoners in Sing Sing was called the "condemned cells" or "CCs." In "The Center," an eight-doored room sitting at the hub of the building, Ray and Martha were led into separate wings of the prison. Marta walked hesitantly through a wooden door into the four-celled wing for women, while Ray "strutted" into the twelve-cell corridor for men.

Constructed of drab brick and stone, the cold, forbidding atmosphere and feeling of confinement of the cells was amplified by the steel bars encasing their windows, but as a woman – and the sole occupant of the women's condemned cells – Martha enjoyed less restraints than Ray. She could leave her cell at nearly any time during the day and could walk around the wing or stroll along the exercise yard at her leisure. She was not; however, allowed to see Ray.

Four days after her arrival at Sing Sing, Martha sat for an interview with the *Daily News*. As music played through a recessed ceiling speaker, she walked into the waiting room of the women's section of the condemned cell block with a "big smile on her heavy face." "Some of These Days," the 1926 version made famous by Sophie Tucker, a singer known as "The Last of the Red-Hot Mamas" because of the tendency of her singing to reflect her hearty sexual appetite, played softly in the background. Martha no doubt appreciated the irony as the lyrics drifting through the stagnant air formed a perfect soundtrack for her current condition of forced separation from Ray:

> *Some of these days*
> *You'll miss me honey*
> *Some of these days*
> *You're gonna be so lonely*
>
> *You'll miss my huggin'*
> *You're gonna miss my kissin'*
> *You're gonna miss me, honey*
> *When I'm far away*
>
> *I feel so lonely*
> *For you only*
> *'Cause you know, honey*
> *You've always had your way*
>
> *And when you leave me*
> *You know it's gonna grieve me*
> *You'll miss your big fat mama*
> *Some of these days.*

Putting on a happy face, Martha assured the reporter and attorney Herbert Rosenberg, who was also present, that the prison staff were treating her well.

"The meals are wonderful," she professed, "and I get all the sleep I want." She lowered her voice slightly as if disclosing a secret. "Not like the other prisons, where the lights used to blind me all night and keep me awake."

Martha acknowledged that she wanted to be able to communicate with Ray, but Sing Sing regulations prohibited it. She could not even write to him.

"Are you lonely here?" Rosenberg asked.

"No, I think it's a cheerful place," Martha said, forcing a faint smile.

She described how she spent her days behind bars.

"I'll find some way to kill time. When they let me go out for exercise, I'll exercise, play handball, or count the bricks in the wall. Something to pass the time away."

One of her favorite activities was listening to the radio.

"I can listen to it all I want," she said happily as she gestured at the speaker.

She boasted how her family had recently sent her a box of candy and some cookies, and she seemed optimistic that the ongoing legal appeal of her conviction would be successful. She also shared that she planned to write a book to raise money for her appeal. She already had a title picked out: "Two Thousand and One." It referred to the fact that she was the only female condemned inmate sharing Sing Sing with nearly 2000 men.

The *Daily News* reporter wanted to meet briefly with Ray as well, so Rosenberg asked Martha one last question.

"Do you miss Raymond?"

Her smile slowly disappeared, replaced by a rigid frown.

"Yes, I miss him now more than ever," she said. "My love for him will never change."

The reporter followed Rosenberg to the men's wing of the condemned cells. Ray had gained weight, and was noticeably heavier after his short time at Sing Sing. Seeing him in that condition depressed Rosenberg. He wanted Ray to know that he had done everything he could in defending him.

"Are you dissatisfied with my representation of you at trial?" he asked.

"No, of course not," Ray replied. "If your summation couldn't save my life, then I'm ready to go," he said in all seriousness.

Ray shared that he was spending much of his time reading law books like the Penal Code.

"Wait until you come up here the next time and I'll tell you more about law than you believe possible," he joked.

"Do you miss Martha?" Rosenberg asked, ending the interview in similar fashion as he did Martha's.

"Terribly," Ray asserted in a melancholy tone. "Please tell her that I miss her terribly."

Rosenberg nodded and assured the condemned man that he would.

"So long," Rosenberg said as he stood to leave.

"So long, for now," Ray replied, putting on a positive front like Martha had. "Some day I'll walk out of here with you," he said half-convincingly.

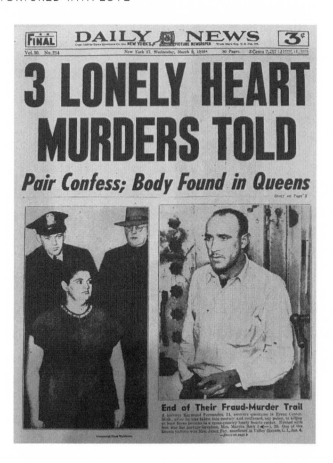

FINAL ★★ **DAILY ☆ NEWS** **3¢**

Vol. 30. No. 214   New York 17, Wednesday, March 2, 1949★   56 Pages   2 Cents

3 LONELY HEART MURDERS TOLD

Pair Confess; Body Found in Queens

Story on Page 3

End of Their Fraud-Murder Trail

A nervous Raymond Fernandez, 34, answers questions in Bronx Center, while, after he was taken into custody and confessed, say police, to killing at least three persons in a cross-country lonely hearts racket. Nabbed with him was his partner-inerime, Mrs. Martha Beck (←), 29. One of the known victims was Mrs. Janet Fay, murdered in Valley Stream, L. I., Jan. 4.

Part Three

You made me think you cared for me
And I believed in you
You told me things you never meant
And made me think them true.

You made me what I am today
I hope you're satisfied
You dragged and dragged me down until
The soul within me died.

"The Curse of An Aching Heart" - Henry Fink 1913

Chapter Twenty-Seven

As Ray and Martha's appeals wound their way through the judicial system, Ray put his letter writing skills to good use. Although segregated in his cell on the condemned wing of the prison, he was not entirely shut off from human contact. He enjoyed weekly, sometimes twice-weekly, visits with his three sisters and brothers-in-law, who often provided money so he could purchase cigars and other items. Like many behind bars, he also turned to religion, attending Mass every Sunday at the prison's Catholic service. Though Martha had less restrictions on her movement in the women's section of condemned cells, her time there also differed from Ray's in that she had virtually no visitors. Only her attorneys came to see her.

The main premise of Ray's appeal contended that Judge Pecora did not adequately consider the impropriety of having one attorney – Herbert Rosenberg – represent two defendants at trial due to the inevitable conflicts of interest. The argument appeared to have merit, particularly since the New York Court of Appeals declined to assign Rosenberg as appellate counsel for both Ray and Martha under that very reasoning, finding that "examination of the record in the trial court apparently shows the interests of the defendant Fernandez to be in conflict with the interests of the defendant Beck to a degree which necessitates that each defendant be represented by independent counsel."

The appellate brief filed by Ray's new attorney asserted that, due to the inherent conflict of interests arising from representation of both Ray and Martha at trial, Rosenberg should have filed a motion for severance at the beginning of the proceedings requesting a separate trial of each defendant. Martha's appeal, filed by Rosenberg, focused largely on the alleged improprieties by prosecutors in promising immunity in exchange for confessions, the purported lack of evidence against Martha, and due process infringement tied to the conditions under which the jury reached its verdict.

For its part, aside from countering the legal arguments advanced by the two defendants, the prosecution's appellate briefs painted Ray as a cold-blooded killer: "When cool, calm and collected action was needed to accomplish his purposes, Fernandez was cool, calm and collected...and he killed when killing appeared necessary." And Martha was his all-too-willing accomplice.

In addition to the two sides' appellate briefs, the voluminous Record on Appeal consisted of seven volumes of trial transcripts comprising more than 4000 pages. The parties presented oral arguments to the New York Court of Appeals on April 3, 1950. Three months later, the court issued its decision affirming both convictions. However, Judge Conway filed a dissenting opinion on grounds the trial judge, Judge Pecora, failed to make reference to the "one issue in the case raised by the defendant Fernandez which, if believed, would have led to his acquittal of the capital offense charged." Specifically, the failure to include in the jury instructions that if Ray did not kill Janet Fay and was instead an accessory after the fact, he could not be found guilty of murder or manslaughter. As another issue warranting a reversal and new trial, Judge Conway also pointed to the existence of a "sharp conflict of interest between the two defendants" while being "represented by the same counsel."

As the appeals process dragged on, letters written to or on behalf of Ray and Martha revealed conflicting perceptions of them. A letter from Ray's sister, Lena Cano, to the Warden of Sing Sing attempted to humanize the woman many thought a monster: *I have been told by Mr. Rosenberg that I cannot write or see Martha under any circumstances....I know she is lonely, and no matter what she did, she is still a human being.* Conversely, a letter from Deliphene Downing's mother a few months later evoked the monstrous side of that human being: *Why this was all done we can't understand....It is just unbelievable that any human could come in our home and be so nice and at the same time know what they were working for at the time and all the false things they told us and Deliphene.*

Similarly, letters written by Ray and Martha provided a peek into their state of mind. In a January 17, 1950 letter to her sister Ronda McDaniel, Martha stated:

> *I have come to the conclusion that to be employed here at Sing Sing you have to either be a Moron or just plain stupid....I can tell you everything that has taken place here...and a lot of that would cause people's ears to burn if they knew I'd written it down. Oh yes, it is a very accurate report. Perhaps some day you can read it – It will all be included in my book under the sub-heading or chapter of "Sing Sing Diary."*

Her August 21 letter to Herbert Rosenberg revealed a dark sense of humor, as she ended the letter with the notation: *Don't forget to send me a 'Happy Anniversary' card – Sing Sing Prison has been <u>Honored</u> with my presence exactly one year tomorrow...Your favorite criminal. Martha*

Chapter Twenty-Eight

As days turned to weeks and weeks turned to months, the seemingly unbreakable bond between Martha and Ray began to weaken with the countless hours of confinement giving rise to a corrosive suspicion. The time behind bars particularly took its toll on Ray. From the limited vantage point of his cell, he became convinced that Martha was having an affair with one of the Sing Sing guards. He became obsessed with the thought and it ate at him more and more until he demanded that his attorney, William Richter, do something. A September 18, 1950 letter to Richter spelled out Ray's grievance:

Due to very unpleasant circumstances that concern undue and entirely unnecessary tension, strain, and mental torture put upon me by a certain Officer and those around him, has led me to such a state of mind and desperation that, I find myself uncapable of standing it much longer without fear of unwillingly and beyond my control to find myself involved in some desperate or violent act upon either the Officer or my own self.

Therefore I sincerely request of you to withdraw my appeal at the U.S. Supreme Court for, if my application should be considered and the Honorable Justices decided to review my case, it would take months before any decision, and I could never stand it under the present circumstances and conditions here.

Shortly thereafter, Richter wrote to the Warden of Sing Sing about the guard in question:

> *I understand this particular guard, a 'Mr. Alford,' has access to both the cell blocks of Martha Beck and Raymond Fernandez. He apparently takes undue liberties with these opportunities, and particularly in tormenting Fernandez, and bearing tales between the inmates Beck and Fernandez, and creating animosity and futility between them.*

The same day, Martha wrote about the alleged affair to her mother, Julia Seabrook:

> *It is all over the prison that I am pregnant. Nice huh? Well, for your information I am not...I think you know who lit the match that caused the flame – He swore he'd make me sorry I'd been born if I ever turned against him – he certainly is trying to stir up animosity against me.*

She later told her sister, Mary Davidson, that Ray must be "trying to escape the death chair by playing crazy."

On September 23, Richter obtained a writ of habeas corpus directing the Warden to bring Ray to federal court. The court filing asserted that Ray was being subjected to "mental torture beyond endurance" by a "sadistic death house triangle" involving Martha and a Sing Sing guard. It alleged that Ray had become suicidal due to the "cruel and unusual punishment" inflicted by a "principal guard stationed at the prison," and that as a result, Ray had asked to withdraw his appeal to the Supreme Court so that he could be executed at once and "escape his living death."

Two days later, Martha fired off a letter to her sister, Vera:

The mails are not fast enough for me to deny the accusations given out (last night on Winchell's radio program) over the air. He said that the affair between me and a prison guard had been confirmed – I wonder who confirmed it – They certainly know more than I do. You would think it was one of these daytime soap operas: Wednesday in Federal Court in New York, the name of the guard will dramatically be revealed. Tune in tomorrow to "Martha's other Love." Don't miss the next absorbing episode in the life of the woman who says, "Who's next, please."

Upon learning of the issuance of the writ, acting Warden Wilfred Denno stated: "It's ridiculous. But you can never tell what goes on in the minds of men in the death house." According to Denno, Ray and Martha were housed in separate blocks of the prison and the "only time Mrs. Beck even sees a male guard is when the shifts change. The rest of the time she is under constant supervision of one or more of the four matrons who are assigned to her section."

Martha took the entire proceeding as an affront to her sense of virtue. The next day, she wrote Denno:

For several weeks I have suffered in silence because of the rumors started by Mr. Ferndandez. After hearing Walter Winchell's 9:00 p.m. broadcast, I feel that I should be allowed to ask for a retraction, apology, or denial of the charge. To print or say that I am having an affair with a guard is one of the most asinine and ridiculous statements ever made. Approximately twenty five million persons (quoting radio) heard Winchell's broadcast tonight.

In an affidavit Martha swore that at no time had she ever been sexually harassed or molested by an employee of the prison, that she was under the constant supervision of a prison matron twenty-four hours a day, and that the only males who had visited her in prison were her attorney and the Protestant Chaplain of Sing Sing. She also sent a letter to her sister expressing her astonishment about the allegations and poking fun at how seriously Ray was taking the situation.

Can this woman, from a small mill town in the south, find happiness in Sing Sing, or will her size prove to her, what so many women have already proved. That men seldom make passes at women who wear glasses. Don't miss Wednesday's absorbing episode when in a crowded courtroom in Federal Court, N.Y.C, the forgotten Lover will take the witness stand and in a dramatic motion will, with shaking finger, and sob-choked voice, point out a prison guard and say "He is the man who stole the affections of the woman I loved." I ask you, how corny can you get?

Did you hear Winchell's statement last night of my affair with the guard? Today's Mirror quoted his lawyer as saying RMF witnesses me and the guard's personal relationship. What evil lurks in the minds of men? As the Shadow – he knows!!!!"

Then she touched on what her relationship with Ray had been like in the past, portraying him as having wielded an unhealthy control over her.

I stopped letting him rule me – and started thinking for myself....Big hearted, loving me, I accepted half the blame – noble of me wasn't it? I was lying to protect him. So what – it's actually worth all this to be free of him – and my old self once again.

After investigating Ray's complaints, the Warden sent his report to the Commissioner of Correction, finding that the love triangle allegations stemmed from Ray's personal dislike of prison guard Roy Alford. The Warden also noted that Ray and Martha had not been on friendly terms for several weeks leading up to the allegations due to Ray becoming vindictive and "blaming everyone but himself" for his conviction and death sentence. The Warden concluded: *there is absolutely no basis for the charge made by Fernandez and this action is either some sort of a cheap publicity stunt to embarrass Mrs. Beck and the Department [of Corrections], or some legal action to try and lay the ground-work as to Fernandez's insanity.*

In another letter, Martha revealed the extent to which Ray's accusations had hurt her.

I'm still a human, feeling every blow inside, even though I have the ability to hide my feelings and laugh. But that doesn't say my heart isn't breaking from the inside and humiliation of being talked about as I am – Oh yes, I wear a cloak of laughter. Lest anyone should see. My dress of sorry underneath, and stop to pity me. I wear a cloak of laughter, lest anyone should guess, that what is hid beneath it, is less than happiness.

The legal maneuvers of the love triangle controversy eventually fizzled out when Ray's attorney dropped the proceedings in mid-October 1950, but by then the damage had already been done. If the allegations and court filing had been a ploy by Ray aimed at overturning his death sentence, then the plan failed entirely. Indeed, its sole effect seemed to be the tearing of a rift in his relationship with Martha. Despite his abandonment of the legal proceeding, Martha lashed out at Ray in a note she wrote to him:

You are a double-crossing, two-timing skunk. It's nice to learn what a terrible murderous person I am, while you are such a misunderstood, white-haired boy, caught in the clutches of a female vampire. It was also nice to know that all of the love letters you wrote "from your heart" were written with a hand shaking with laughter at me for being such a gullible fool to believe them.

Chapter Twenty-Nine

While Martha experienced prison-house relationship woes with Ray, her attorney Herbert Rosenberg was dealing with his own marital problems. He hinted at the trouble in a September 22 letter to Martha, telling her:

> *I got a little detail on my own personal matter to straighten out next week, and after that, I'll have a little more time....By the way, do you know any mother-in-law jokes? That's one thing you ought to be lucky and thankful for – that you don't have a mother-in-law, at least at this stage of the proceeding.*

A month later, Rosenberg settled a lawsuit that his wife, Rosemary, had filed against him for a legal accounting concerning $50,000 she had entrusted to him following their 1946 marriage. In her suit, she alleged that Rosenberg had pressured her into giving him control of the funds, and that he was supposed to manage them on behalf of her eight-year-old son from her former marriage.

After the marriage, Rosemary's court filing stated, *my husband proceeded to bring pressure on me to influence me unduly in various ways to turn over the property to him. In 1947, while I was seriously ill*

*in Johns Hopkins Hospital in Baltimore, my husband by undue influ-
ence and improper pressure prevailed upon me to sign over my property to him.*

In his response, Rosenberg counterclaimed for a half-interest in her
family's 1,000-acre ranch holdings worth $5,000,000, claiming that the
wealthy heiress – whose family traced the roots of its oil wells, cattle
ranches, and orange groves all the way back to original Spanish land
grants – had given him the money as a gift.

But while Rosenberg and his wife bitterly ended their relationship,
Ray and Martha began the process of repairing theirs. Time heals all
wounds, and its slow passage behind bars eventually relieved the sting
and soothed the hurt feelings caused by the alleged prison love triangle. Writing in response to an angry note from Ray in which he had
lashed out by telling her not to write him anymore, Martha initiated the
reconciliation process: *Under the present circumstances I know you
will accept this note and forgive me for writing. I just want you to know
that I don't hate you, and that I never will. Life is too short for me,
now, to hate or feel bitter.*

Both had been cast as the black sheep of their families before Fate
brought them together to share a life of sin, and now the two tortured
souls found each other again, reconciling their strange romance that
seemed fated to endure to the end.

Chapter Thirty

With the first days of the new year came the growing realization that Ray and Martha would not escape a date with the electric chair. That reality hit home on January 17, 1951, when the New York Court of Appeals upheld their death sentences and set their execution for the week of March 5. Following standard procedure, but feeling to Ray and Martha more like salt being poured in the wound, the Warden sent them both official notice of the event on January 22: *I am sorry to inform you that I am in receipt of an Order of the Court of Appeals, fixing the week of March 5, 1951, as the date for carrying into effect, the original sentence of death in your case.*

But few felt bad for the two of them. A letter from Deliphene Downing's mother sent to the pair a month after the denial of their appeal left no doubt about her feelings on the matter:

I do feel sorrow for your parents and relatives, that you brought these crimes into their lives. I will say this, the chair is too easy for you. You should be tortured like you did Mrs. Fay and poor Deliphene and our Doll of Rainelle. Martha Beck, how could you or any human take a sweet innocent baby and do what you did to her? I am sure you will not dread the chair for there is no heart in people like you.

I know we will never meet in heaven for there is no room in heaven for people like you. Hell has plenty of room and is waiting for you.

Reflecting the public sentiment favoring an eye for an eye, a Sing Sing administrator reported that "[d]uring recent weeks hundreds of requests for invitations have poured in, many from women, some of whom bluntly said they'd like to pull the switch themselves on Martha." Reflecting the tenure of the time, Warden William Synder pointed out that the applications were being consistently turned down because women "don't make proper witnesses."

Meanwhile, Martha began preparing herself for what was to come, setting what affairs she could in order, including signing a statement donating her eyes to the Eye-Bank for Sight Restoration, pushing Herbert Rosenberg out of her affairs, and looking into the possibility of providing for the children she had abandoned years earlier so she could stay with Ray. On February 5, she wrote the editor of the *New York Journal* following up an inquiry that the journal had made about buying the rights to her story.

If we should come to any terms, the check offered for my material is to be made payable to my mother, for my children, not to Herbert Rosenberg. There would have to be some agreement or contract, however, that the material would not be deleted, to protect Herbert Rosenberg, as my material will expose him as being an unorthodox, scheming, shyster, and your readers would have a first-hand picture of the lengths he went for free publicity.

In a February 28 letter to her sister she shared her still-simmering resentment of Ray over his handling of her alleged affair with the prison guard:

You don't know how scared some people are – especially of death – It takes a man to walk to it – I wonder – how many men will it take to drag a SKUNK there...[T]hat damn fool woman in VT had given Ray the letter I'd written to her – telling her that he was after her money –

*how he had married other women etc. She didn't appreciate it
however – gave him the letter. He came back and tried to kill me –
Remember when I was there I told you how he knocked my teeth
loose, hitting me in the mouth with his fist. Then he choked me
unconscious....Keep your chin up – I'll try to blow a fuse.*

She also compared Ray to Herbert Rosenberg, telling her sister that
the only difference in him and Rosenberg *is that Rosemary [Rosen-
berg's wife] is still alive.*

On Friday, March 2, Ray and Martha learned the exact date of their
death. The Warden scheduled their executions for Thursday, March 8,
giving them less than a week to live. As part of his logistical preparations, the Warden sent a short note to Joseph Francel of Cairo, New
York, the official executioner of Sing Sing, advising him: *I shall expect
you to be here at the usual time that day.*

Francel took over as official executioner for the State of New York
in 1939. His predecessor, Robert Elliott, oversaw 387 executions while
serving as executioner for New York and five other states from 1926
until his death in 1939. He developed the standard electrocution procedure of applying 2000 volts for three seconds, 500 for 57 seconds,
2000 for another three seconds, 500 for another 57 seconds, and then a
final few seconds of 2000 volts again. Elliott's designed his technique
to instantly render the condemned prisoner unconscious with the first
massive shock, while the longer, lower voltage shocks killed by
roasting the vital organs, and the oscillating cycle of shocks stopped
the victim's heart. Toward the end of his tenure as executioner, Elliott
denounced the death penalty, asserting that the "happiest day I'll ever
experience...will be the day that capital punishment is wiped from the
statute books, leaving me without any more business, a man out of a
job." Shortly before he died, Elliott wrote *Agent of Death: The
Memoirs of an Executioner*, which concludes: *I hope that the day is not
far distant when legal slaying, whether by electrocution, hanging,
lethal gas, or any other method is outlawed throughout the United
States.*

On the last Sunday of her life, Martha spent much of the day praying in solitude, seeing only the Reverend Luther Hannum, the Protestant chaplain of Sing Sing, who conducted a service exclusively for her using a portable altar.

At a special appeal session convened in the Death House, Martha listened with exasperation as her lawyers explained the latest setback in her appeals and their recommended strategy for continuing the process further. She eventually eyed her lawyers with annoyance and announced that she wanted to withdraw her appeal. She would no longer try to avoid her date with the electric chair.

"There's one difference between you and me," she told her attorneys facetiously, "I know what I'm doing."

With no future of her own, Martha's thoughts turned towards her children's future. Perhaps regretting her past, Martha also wrote a letter to Dr. Richard Hoffmann, her defense team's chief medical expert during trial who also assisted with her appeal and helped her cope with prison life.

> *Will you be so kind as to write my mother and advise her how and what to tell my children about me? My daughter will be six in Sept., and will also start school the same month. You know, Dr. H., she already has two strikes against her and if I go to the chair it will be strike three. I feel that you are in a position to know how to tell her so that her little mind can grasp the truth and not be warped by all of the malicious jeers and gossip that she will have to face in the future.*

From his lonely cell, Ray watched the Reverend Thomas Donovan, Catholic chaplain of the prison, conduct Mass several yards away. Ray's time in Sing Sing revealed a heart large enough to love two women at once, or so empty as to callously fool one or both of them. In addition to riding his roller coaster relationship with Martha, he rekindled his relationship with Encarnacion Robles, his first wife still living in Spain. Writing from his condemned cell, Prisoner Number 108595 reached out to his wife on September 5, 1949, penning a letter in Spanish addressed to her at the Hotel Principe Alfonso in Cadiz, Spain:

Encarna:

I know this letter will come as a great surprise. But I have decided to write and tell you that my wishes are that when you receive this letter you, our three sons, and daughter are all in perfect health. For the moment, I am doing well.

I know you've heard about everything that's happened to me. I shall not be surprised if you do not write me any longer. I presume you have read in the newspapers that I have been sentenced to die in the electric chair.

I had a talk with Lena and she told me that she is arranging to have you and the children brought to America. If that happens, I do not think I will be alive to see you and the children. However, if it occurs that way, I shall be happy because if the price of your coming to America to live a happy life is my own life, then I am glad to give it. After all, I have suffered and struggled so much in this world without any benefits, that it will be good to die. In regard to what brought me into this trouble, there is little I can say, as I still do not know how I got mixed up in it. Everything took place so quickly, that sometimes I think I am dreaming.

Ecstatic to receive a letter from her in reply, Ray quickly wrote to her again, expressing his relief that she still cared for him: *Darling, you cannot imagine how glad your letter made me. You say that you have read all that the newspapers have written, but that you do not believe it. Believe me, that has been my only worry since I've been here, but now I realize that you still have faith in me.* Ray also mentioned some letters that he claimed would exonerate him: *My immediate family not only believe in my innocence, they have certain letters that prove that I am innocent. I want you to keep those letters and show them to the children when they are grown up and understand what life is, so they can see their father was not so mean as the papers and the public insist.* Whatever information they contained, the referenced letters never surfaced in the courts or in the press, and were not otherwise made public.

In an undated letter translated by the Sing Sing correspondence department, Encarnacion wrote to Ray of her undying devotion: *It is my great desire to be with you. My thoughts never have been far away from you. I will never forget you as long as I live.* She declined his suggestion of selling his life story to help support her and their four children: *I don't want you to write the history of your life for money. I don't want that kind of money and I would prefer to go hungry then to get money from a book that would tell about your life. Think of all this as a dream.*

Ray's letters revealed a fervent wish to explain to his wife how he had ended up in Sing Sing, but an inability to do so, as if he himself could not understand the course of events. On October 5, 1949, he wrote:

> *If you believe what the newspapers in New York have been saying, you might think that I am the worst human being in the world. But I am consoled by the fact that...you know that I am not a bad man. My only weakness has been women, which in a way have dominated me...Lena will show you letters written by me and another person and you will be convinced that if I die, it has been by trying to do a favor to someone else. Although you may think that I am a fool in doing so, but remember that my mother was a woman, you are a woman, and I have a daughter who some day will grow to be a woman, and I have sisters. What does it mean if I, one who rates nothing, dies protecting a woman. If I cannot make it, at least I shall do my best not to be a coward.*

In a subsequent letter, he wrote: *It is so difficult for me to think how I got in this trouble. I tried to do good to others thinking that I was not going to get in trouble.*

On Halloween 1949, Ray wrote to his Spanish wife in a reflective mood, contemplating how his upbringing might have influenced his criminal behavior and shedding some insight about the nature of his relationship with Martha.

> *I cannot help thinking over and over, and the more I think I realize that if my father had been different all of this would not have happened. But what can you do, life is a mystery that nobody seems to understand. Only God knows all. I shall tell you that all day long I am thinking of you, what you are doing and how you are feeling and if I will ever see and embrace you again....There is no doubt that I love you from the bottom of my heart, that nothing or nobody will make it fade, but this woman who is here with me, I love her, but it is a pitiful love I have for her. I hope that little by little I shall forget it, and I also hope that you will forgive me for saying this to you, but I know you always expected me to say the truth....Please forgive what I said in regard to the other woman. Goodbye my darling, I love you and shall love you always.*

Later, he wrote that he had been a fool for allowing himself to get mixed up with Martha: *I realize how stupid I was when I thought there could be another woman to take your place in my heart...and for me to believe in a woman who has no heart and no feelings.*

Encarnacion was eager to blame Martha for Ray's downfall too. Despite everything, she still saw him as the hard working, humble man that she had married. *I cannot believe that you have done what the newspapers say about you,* she wrote on January 10, 1950, *as nobody better than I knows how good-hearted and kind you have always been to everybody. It is that bad woman who dragged you to the place where you are now.*

Writing on their wedding anniversary, Encarnacion reflected on Ray's current state and concluded that his troubles were simply the result of allowing himself to associate with the wrong people, namely Martha.

If I would have been with you, I am sure nothing would have happened because your wife and children would have been with you and that woman would not have been in your way. I understand that a lonely man is liable to do anything when he meets a charming woman. He may lose his head. But all women are not alike. Some of us live only for our children and husbands. Others live for divorces, pleasures, and to break other homes.

On January 8, 1951, signing as "Ramon," Ray told Encarnacion that he thought his execution would be in February. Although he assured her that he would *not give up hope*, he closed the letter by pledging: *You are my love and my only love and you always will be.* A week later, he informed her of the date he would be executed, but reminded her not to worry or feel sorrow since he would be *going out of this world very happy.* Ray put on a brave face for his wife, writing that he had *suffered so much the last months that death will be a blessing,* and telling her that she should not worry about him *as I am awaiting here something that will mean my rest from so many troubles.*

In her final letter, Encarnacion assured her condemned husband that *if you have done something to me I always pardoned you with my heart.* She concluded by sending him *love from the one who will never forget you.* The same date that Encarnacion wrote her letter, Ray penned a letter to his brothers expressing acceptance of his fate: *Death is a thing I have no fear of and am not worried about. At the end we all have to die, and if it is my destiny and the wishes of God for it to be this way, what can we do?*

Chapter Thirty-One

On Wednesday, March 7, Martha and Ray had their last hour in the sun. Both displayed the resigned acceptance that often overtakes condemned prisoners on the eve of their execution. Ray burned off anxious energy by playing handball against a wall in the prison exercise yard. Martha spent her hour in a more subdued mood, quietly walking around the yard before spending a sleepless night in the darkness of her cell.

The next morning, Ray and Martha were moved to separate sections of the "Dance Hall," the special pre-execution chamber where Sing Sing's condemned spent their last day. Martha requested a finger wave hairstyle to prepare for her date with the electric chair. She dabbed rouge to her lips and cheeks, then checked her appearance by peering into a small mirror. For her last meal, she ate fried chicken, French fries, and a lettuce and tomato salad. She declined dessert.

As she collected some thoughts in a contemplative frame of mind, Martha told the prison chaplain: "I know my sin was great, but the penalty is great, too. That makes things even, I guess. I don't think I need to fear what lies ahead."

Meanwhile, in his wing of the Dance Hall, Ray had a last meal of an onion omelet, sliced tomatoes, apples, pears, almond-flavored ice cream, and coffee. Afterward, he enjoyed smoking a Cuban cigar. Informed that his final appeal had been denied, Ray seemed to take the news in stride.

"If I have to die, I'm ready," he said stoically. "That's something I've been prepared for since 1949, so tonight I'll die like the man nobody thinks I am."

As the appointed hour drew near, prison officials shaved a round spot the size of a silver dollar on the tops of the two condemned prisoners' heads. It was normal pre-execution procedure to facilitate contact with the electric chair's deadly electrode. At 9:00 p.m., only two hours before the time set for their execution, the condemned lovers were allowed to exchange messages. In her final moments, the recent hurtful times with Ray passed away and Martha penned a poem declaring her love for him:

> *Remember, Sweetheart, the night when you and I*
> *Side by side were sitting*
> *Watching o'er the moonlit sky.*
> *Fleecy clouds flitting*
> *How close our hands*
> *were linked then.*
> *When, my darling, when*
> *will they be linked again?*
> *What to me the starlight still*
> *Or the moonbeams' splendor,*
> *If I do not feel the thrill*
> *Of your fingers tender?*

Ray received Martha's poem from Herbert Rosenberg with the nervous look of a groom waiting for his bride to walk down the aisle on their wedding day. After reading Martha's tender expression, Ray burst into a relieved smile.

"I want to shout my love for you to the world!" he exclaimed as if the emotional weight of his words would knock down the walls so Martha could hear them. "I'm going to die like a man. What the hell does the public know about love? The news brought to me that Martha loves me is the best I've had in years. Now I'm ready to die."

With a sad, yet joyous heart, he wrote Martha a short reply pledging his undying love. Martha read his note with true contentment in her eyes. She knew that their love would endure even beyond death. Now that all was again right with the light of her life, Martha had just one more message to deliver. Before being led to the death chamber, she gave Herbert Rosenberg a final statement for publication by the press:

My last statement to my attorney is that I have sinned and society will know that I am paying this debt. The sin is great and so is the penalty. This is not the minute to speak of who is to blame. What is in the past must remain in the past.

My story is a love story, but only those tortured by love can know what I mean. I was pictured as a fat, unfeeling woman. True I am fat. But if that were a crime, how many of my sex would be guilty? I am not without feeling. I am a woman who has had a great love and always will have.

Prisons and the death house have only strengthened my feeling for Raymond. In the history of the world, how many crimes have been attributed to love?

Here are my last words and my last thought:

"Let he who is without sin cast the first stone."

"I love Raymond."

Sporting his signature bow-tie and standing outside Sing Sing's imposing barbed-wire topped chain-link fence, Herbert Rosenberg addressed a group of men huddled around him wearing fedoras and thick overcoats. With tired eyes, he told the assembly of reporters that Martha had offered to donate her body to science if the state would spare her lover. But this eleventh-hour expression of Martha's devotion to Ray did nothing to sway his executioners. Rosenberg's clemency petition to Governor Thomas Dewey asking the Governor to "remember the children," Martha's son and daughter, had similarly failed. In denying the clemency request, Dewey sternly replied that he did remember the children, especially little Rainell Downing who Martha had so monstrously drowned in a basement laundry basin.

At 11:12 p.m., Ray walked the "Last Mile" through the corridor that connected the Dance Hall ante-room to the cold, barren room of the Sing Sing death chamber. The chamber's dolorous color reflected its dismal atmosphere. The walls were dark green at their lower portion, bordered by black, then pale yellow at the upper parts. Accompanied by the prison's Catholic priest and flanked by a handful of guards, Ray shuffled through the green door directly facing the electric chair and stared intently around the small room with "sparkling" eyes. The Warden, twelve official witnesses, two doctors, various additional observants, and the official executioner known as the "State Electrician" were waiting for him in the execution chamber.

As guards positioned Ray onto the chair, he carefully pulled up his black pants to preserve the crease, an automatic habit now pointless in purpose, but a powerfully human act lending a "strange, grim dignity to death." Witnesses noticed the "suggestion of a smile at the corners of his mouth" while five guards buckled black leather straps around his limbs and torso to secure him. The State Electrician, Joseph Francel, stepped forward and checked the electrode and sponge strapped to Ray's right leg. Satisfied about their condition, he slid a leather helmet containing another electrode over Ray's head, then connected a cable and secured the electrode flush against his skin. Just before the executioner wrapped the black leather mask around his face, Ray kissed a crucifix offered by the priest. The death mask fitted firmly in place, Francel stepped to the left of the chair and into an alcove adjacent to the death chamber. He took position by the switchboard that controlled the electrical current to the chair.

Upon the Warden's signal, Francel flipped a lever sending the first surge of deadly electricity into Ray's body. As the lights throughout Sing Sing flickered, Ray's body tightened in reaction to 2000 volts of electricity shooting into his leg and head, relaxing only when the executioner cut the power. Someone in the crowded room of witnesses dropped a pencil that, in the terrible silence of the moment, sounded like a bell clanging when it struck the floor. Ray's involuntary movements shifted in cadence to the electrical current as if maintaining a macabre rhythm with the deadly charge while it rose and fell. The ghastly dance repeated several more times until the executioner was satisfied his job was done. After double-checking that the electrical current had been cut, Sing Sing's chief surgeon leaned over Ray's slumped body to check his vital signs with a stethoscope.

"I pronounce this man dead," he said following a few moments of unpleasant silence, establishing the time of legal electrocution as 11:16 p.m.

Asked if execution by legal electrocution was any better than murder, the Warden's predecessor, Lewis Lawes, replied, "As if one crime of such nature, done by a single man, acting individually, can be expiated by a similar crime done by all men, acting collectively."

Though he shared Judge Pecora's personal opposition to the electric chair, the warden followed his duty in carrying out legally sanctioned death sentences just as the judge had adhered to his duty in imposing them.

As guards wheeled Ray's body into the autopsy room adjacent to the execution chamber, another guard informed the matron watching Martha in her holding cell that it was time.

"It's time to go, Martha" the matron told her. Despite herself, she had come to like Martha. During their hours together a friendship of sorts had developed so there was some genuine sadness in her voice. And with her words a look of sadness spread across Martha's face.

"That means Ray is already gone," Martha remarked in almost a whisper.

She wiped a tear from her eye, trying to take solace in the fact that she and Ray would soon be together forever. She took a deep breath and stood up.

"What the hell are we waiting for?" she told the matron.

At 11:24 p.m., Martha entered the execution room with a "quiet dignity," wearing a blue-gray frock in place of the bright flowered dress she had worn earlier in the day. Along with the usual contingent of guards, a matron clad in white walked in front of her and Protestant Reverend Luther Hannum walked at her side, but Martha did not address him or even glance his way as he quietly recited a prayer. Instead, she looked around the room, scanning the faces of the nearly three dozen witnesses crammed into the "chapel-like pews" of the death chamber. She recognized arresting officers Clarence Randall and James Toohey, Charles Hildebrandt, and other detectives who had investigated the Janet Fay homicide. No doubt she would have bristled to learn that in their letter to the Warden requesting two passes to witness the execution, Randall and Toohey had written: "We had the pleasure of bringing this pair to justice, and would appreciate your kind consideration allowing us to see the finish of two blood thirsty people."

It took Martha a few moments of wiggling to squeeze into the ominous wooden chair. As soon as she was seated, guards stepped forward and fit straps around her arms and body. As Reverend Hannum read the Twenty-third Psalm, quietly murmuring, "The Lord is my Shepherd, I shall not want," a slight smile appeared on Martha's lips. She looked at the matron beside her and winked.

"So long," Martha said faintly.

She glanced up as the black, death mask was lowered over her head, then sat silent and motionless except for the slight movement of her breathing. "Have mercy on me, oh Lord," Hannum murmured on her behalf just before the executioner threw the switch, sending the first of four shocks of electricity into her body. The witnesses watched as she "struggled and strained against the straps" during the first shock, accompanied by the faint hum of the electric current coursing through her body. When the second shock surged through her, Martha's hands clenched tightly, she jerked forward, and her body buckled. She was still for the third and fourth jolts. The surgeon stepped forward and placed his stethoscope on her chest.

"I pronounce this woman dead," he announced at 11:24 p.m.

Martha was the thirteenth woman executed by the State of New York, the seventh to die by electrocution. She was thirty-one years old.

At 11:30 p.m., Harold Kipp, Senior Physician of Sing Sing, performed an autopsy of Ray. *The body lies on the table in the usual position after execution: head back, mouth open, eyes staring, right leg drawn up in about half-flexion,* he wrote, including the same language as used in other autopsy reports for electrocutions. He noted the tattoo on Ray's right forearm: "Encarna" on top of a heart with an arrow passing through it inscribed with "Ramon."

Dr. Kipp conducted Martha's autopsy immediately afterward at 11:45 p.m. He listed the official Cause of Death as Legal Electrocution, noting a body weight of 280 pounds. He recorded the same description of Martha's body as he did for Ray, though for Martha he added: *There are the usual seared marks over the nape of the neck and on the right leg just below the knee.*

Pursuant to her donation wishes, Kipp removed both of Martha's eyes and sent them to the Eye-Bank for Sight Restoration. Perhaps with some irony, he recorded that the 400-gram heart of this Lonely Hearts Killer *was not of normal size.*

Who sent you here? Just when my heart was torn.
And tortured with love's latest agony,
When to myself I solemnly had sworn
To walk life's way alone you come to me
With those big eyes, mysterious and strange,
And sad, sweet face, as solemn as the grave.

– Cy Warman 1892

Afterword

The day after their executions, the Warden of Sing Sing sent a simple telegram to the Governor of New York: *Raymond Martinez Fernadez, #108595, and Martha Jule Beck, #108594, were executed last night in conformity with the law.*

Martha's mother claimed her body in the prison morgue and arranged for its shipment to the Waters & Hibbert Funeral Home in Pensacola for burial. Shortly after sunrise on the morning of March 12, Martha's mother and siblings attended a simple service as she was buried beside her father in Milton Cemetery. The multi-murderer took her final resting place among former citizens of her hometown including its first doctor, county officials, educators, and a veteran of the Revolutionary War.

The *Milton Gazette*, the newspaper where Martha had spent many hours watching her father work, published a respectful account of her body's return home for burial:

What forces brought to bear on her life and character, making it possible for her to become a hardened criminal, will never be known....Her greatest mistake, however, seems to have been made as a result of a practical joke when she began to correspond with

Raymond Fernandez through a "lonely hearts club." With him she began a tour of misdeeds which assured her a position in the annals of American crime and two years of suspense and unwelcomed notoriety for her friends and relatives in West Florida.

There could be no explanation for the brutal crimes committed by the pair as the swindled money from lonely women and killed to wipe out suspicion...but people here-abouts will long remember the Milton High School graduate, shy, quiet, studious and lonely, who chose a life of distorted evil rather than the one of service and accomplishment for which she spent years in training.

Ray's sister, Lena Cano, claimed his body. His final resting place is unknown.

Like many other newspapers, the *New York Journal American* printed Ray and Martha's final statements as well as some of their prison love letters, including one from Ray in which he wrote that the romantic love he shared with Martha was the "most potent force in the world."

In February 1953, Julia Seabrook and Dudley Seabrook filed separate libel lawsuits in Escambia County Court against the publisher of a short book about the Lonely Hearts murders. Contending that the book contained false, malicious, and libelous information, the two suits sought damages of $250,000.

Six months later in August, Joseph Francel, the New York State Electrician who had executed Ray and Martha, resigned from his duties. He cited low pay ($150 per execution) and bad publicity as the reasons for his retirement.

Speculating on the significance of the injury caused by the tanker's hatch door that fell on Ray's head in 1945, a prison psychiatric report discussed the three-inch scar on his head running "over the bregma which is the line of the skull separating the occipital or forepart from the remainder of the skull" and covering a "depressed fracture about one-half inch in width." The report noted:

> recent medical studies have disclosed that the frontal lobes of the brain control the executive functions of the mind in which are bound up the self-control potentialities of the individual and that complex group of reactions which are comprised roughly under the name of conscience....[T]he obviously serious skull fracture suffered by Fernandez in 1945 may have injured the frontal lobes of the brain to such an extent that while there is no neurological evidence resulting of a tangible physical nature, he may have suffered an alteration of personality to such an extent that his moral judgment was impaired. Thus, while legally sane, with the power of reason unimpaired, he may have become a moral monster.

In August 1954, criminal psychiatrist Frederic Wertham revealed that he had been asked by Herbert Rosenberg to examine Ray and Martha for purposes of aiding in the preparation of their insanity defense for trial.

"I examined them and unearthed a great deal about their lives," he said. "Especially in the case of Martha Beck, I tried my best to find medical evidence that I could recognize as symptoms of disease and not as signs of personality. I could not find any. The motive of naked greed overshadowed anything else."

On September 6, 1955, Arnold Pigorsh, in his new position as Sheriff of Kent County, oversaw the destruction of a "crate crammed with evidence," all of the evidence the Sheriff's department had gathered in its investigation of the murders of Deliphene and Rainelle Downing.

Although the Downing murders were never prosecuted, their families – and those of Jane Wilson, Myrtle Young, and unknown others – hopefully gained closure and a sense of justice through the Lonely Hearts Killers' convictions and sentences in the Janet Fay case tried in New York.

Julia Metts Seabrook, the overbearing mother who may have been a contributing cause of Martha Beck's tragic slide into crime, died in July 1956. She was buried with her family members in Milton Cemetery.

Martha's brother, Dudley, who raped her as a teenager, joined the Pensacola Police Department in April 1948. In October 1961, he was arrested along with eight other city policemen in connection with a string of burglaries of Pensacola businesses. After being charged with two counts of being an accessory to burglary of a J.J. Newberry & Co. five and dime store, Dudley was suspended from the police force pending disposition of the criminal charges. The charges were eventually dropped in March 1963, and after a ten-hour hearing Dudley was reinstated to the police department in June of that year. In July 1977, Sergeant Dudley Seabrook retired after serving nearly 30 years as a Pensacola policeman. He lived to the ripe old age of 86 and died in November 2002.

In a "freak boating accident" on March 30, 1962, Herbert Rosenberg fell from his 28-foot skiff, the "Three Sons," when the boat was suddenly hit broadside by a large wave. Despite the heroics of another man on board who dove in to rescue hm and bring him back on board, the 52-year-old Rosenberg drowned in the Jones Beach inlet.

Edward Robinson, the chief prosecutor at the Lonely Hearts Killers' trial, went on to become a Supreme Court Justice, elected with the endorsement of both the Republican and Democrat parties in Nassau County. He retired from the bench in 1968 and died two years later at the age of 70.

In 2019, the Library of Congress selected, *Gaslight*, the defining film of Charles Boyer's career, for preservation in the United States National Film Registry due to its cultural, historical, or aesthetic significance.

Due to the limited reach of forensic science at the time, investigators could only conclusively tie Ray and Martha to five murders. However, reports from various states indicated that there were an unknown number of other victims, as well as countless others not killed, but too ashamed of their involvement in soliciting love through the mail to come forward and admit that they had been fleeced by the Lonely Hearts Killers.

Subsequent to Ray and Martha's execution, *True Crime Detective* published a story about Dr. Richard Hoffmann's involvement in their trial. In the article titled, "The Untold Story of Martha," Dr. Hoffmann claimed that Martha was a "victim of physical and psychopathic abnormalities which she could not understand nor cope with, and which finally drove her to become literally the slave of the man who finally destroyed her." He regretted that, due to New York law, he had not been permitted to testify at trial about the full extent of his psychiatric findings about Martha.

"She was not capable of knowing the nature and quality of her acts.

By the legal definition of insanity, she was insane," Hoffmann asserted. Conversely, Ray was a "sadist" who "delighted in gory details, stories of mutilation and rape" from his WWII days.

Insisting that Martha was a psychopath incapable of distinguishing right from wrong, Hoffmann stated that it was actually Ray alone who killed Janet Fay. Martha had taken responsibility for the crime out of a combination of love for Ray and fear of him.

"She was terribly afraid of him," Hoffmann explained. "She thought he could kill her from a distance, kill her in open court. She said over and over, 'Don't tell Ray. He'll kill me!'" Fear, love, and hate all played a part. You can't separate one from the other."

He reiterated the point Herbert Rosenberg had made in his closing argument at trial: that the hammer blow which fractured Janet Fay's skull had to have been inflicted by a right-handed person, and while Martha was left-handed, Ray was right-handed. According to Hoffmann, Ray brought the hammer to the apartment the night that Janet died "with premeditated murder in his mind."

Hoffmann produced a document that he identified as Martha's final confession, which she gave to him shortly before her execution at Sing Sing.

Dr. Hoffmann –

Ray must have heard the argument between Janet and I, for when she slapped me, he prevented us from having a free-for-all. He told me to go back to bed, that he wanted to talk to Janet. I left the room crying and threw myself on the bed, and to drown out my crying I buried my face in my pillow. Some minutes later Ray called to me and the sound of his voice frightened me as he sounded frightened. I ran into the room and was horrified at the sight.

Ray was standing over Mrs. Fay with both hands around her neck. Blood was flowing all over the place from her head and she was moaning faintly. I ran over to him and said, 'My God, Ray, stop that!' He said, "This moaning is driving me crazy!" With those words he dropped her head back on the floor and jerked a neck scarf off a chair and put it around her neck. He put the hammer in the knot and tightened it until the scarf broke.

By this time I was trying to talk some sense to him but he told me to shut up. He then took another scarf off the chair and put it around her neck. He told me to hold the hammer. I said, "Why? She's dead. Why did you kill her?" Then and only then do I believe that he realized what he had done because he sat down on a couch and said, "My God! My God! What have I done?"

I did not strike Janet Fay with a hammer. Neither did I have anything to do with killing her. I never killed anyone in my life.

According to Hoffmann, he showed the confession to Ray, who admitted it to be true, and although Hoffman pleaded with him to confess, Ray refused.

"It's all true, every bit of it," Ray said, flashing a peculiar smile that Hoffman found unpleasant. "But if I go to the chair, Martha goes too."

About the Author

JT Hunter is a true crime author with over fifteen years of experience as a lawyer, including criminal law and appeals. He also has significant training in criminal investigation techniques. When not working on his books, JT is a college professor and enjoys teaching fiction and nonfiction in his creative writing classes.

JT is the bestselling author of *The Devil In The Darkness*, *A Monster of All Time: The True Story of Danny Rolling - The Gainesville Ripper,* and *The Vampire Next Door: The True Story of the Vampire Rapist.*

You can learn more about JT and his other books at www.jthunter.org

A Note From The Author

Thank you for reading *Tortured With Love*. Your support means a lot to me!

If you've enjoyed this book, I would be very grateful if you'd take a few minutes to write a brief review on whatever platform you purchased it from.

Reviews are one of the most powerful tools when it comes to book ranking, exposure, and future sales. I have some loyal readers, and honest reviews of my books help bring them to the attention of new readers.

Thank you so much,
JT

Also by J.T. Hunter

Don't miss some of JT Hunter's other True Crime Accounts!

DEVIL IN THE DARKNESS: The True Story of Serial Killer Israel Keyes

He was a hard-working small business owner, an Army veteran, an attentive lover, and a doting father. But he was also something more, something sinister. A master of deception, he was a rapist, arsonist, bank robber, and a new breed of serial killer, one who studied other killers to perfect his craft. In multiple states, he methodically buried kill-kits containing his tools of murder years before returning and putting them to use. Viewing the entire country as his hunting grounds, he often flew to distant locations where he rented cars and randomly selected his victims. Such were the methods and madness of serial killer Israel Keyes. Such were the demands of the "Devil in the Darkness."

This book is the first detailed account ever published about Israel Keyes. It contains exclusive personal information about this frightening serial killer gleaned from extensive interviews with his former fiancee.

Optioned May 2018 by a Major Production company to be made into a motion picture.

A MONSTER OF ALL TIME: The True Story of Danny Rolling -
the Gainesville Ripper

Ambitious, attractive, and full of potential, five young college students prepared for the new semester. They dreamed of beginning careers and starting families. They had a lifetime of experiences in front of them. But death came without warning in the dark of the night. Brutally ending five promising lives, leaving behind three gruesome crime scenes, the Gainesville Ripper terrorized the University of Florida, casting an ominous shadow across a frightened college town.

What evil lurked inside him? What demons drove him to kill? What made him "A Monster of All Time"?

IN COLDER BLOOD: On the Trail of Dick Hickock and Perry Smith

Two families, mysteriously murdered under similar circumstances, just a month apart. One was memorialized in Truman Capote's classic novel, *In Cold Blood.* The other was all but forgotten.

Dick Hickock and Perry Smith confessed to the first: the November 15, 1959 murder of a family of four in Holcomb, Kansas. Despite remarkable coincidences between the two crimes, they denied committing the second: the December 19 murder of a family of four in Osprey, Florida.

Over half a century later, a determined Florida detective undertakes exceptional efforts to try to bring closure to the long-cold case.

THE COUNTRY BOY KILLER: The True Story of Cody Legebokoff

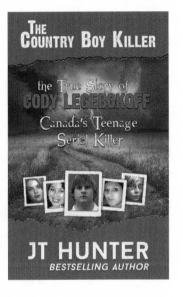

He was the friendly, baby-faced Canadian boy next door. He came from a loving, caring, and well-respected family. Blessed with good looks and back-woods charm, he was popular with his peers and he excelled in sports. A self-proclaimed "die hard" Calgary Flames fan, he played competitive junior hockey and competed on his high school's snowboarding team. And he enjoyed the typical pleasures of a boy growing up in the country: camping, hunting, and fishing with family and friends. But he also enjoyed brutally murdering women, and he became one of the youngest serial killers in Canadian history.

THE VAMPIRE NEXT DOOR: The True Story of the Vampire Rapist

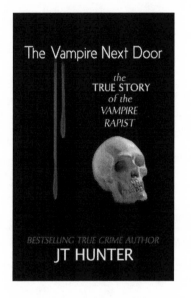

John Crutchley seemed to be living the American Dream. Good-looking and blessed with a genius level IQ, he had a prestigious, white-collar job at a prominent government defense contractor, where he held top secret security clearance and handled projects for NASA and the Pentagon. To all outward appearances, he was a hard-working, successful family man with a lavish new house, a devoted wife, and a healthy young son. But, he concealed a hidden side of his personality, a dark secret tied to a hunger for blood and the overriding need to kill.

As one of the most prolific serial killers in American history, Crutchley committed at least twelve murders, and possibly nearly three dozen. His IQ elipsed that of Ted Bundy, and his body count may have as well. While he stalked the streets hunting his unsuspecting victims, the residents of a quiet Florida town slept soundly, oblivious to the dark creature in their midst, unaware of the vampire next door.

Selected Bibliography

1. Appellate briefs filed by the parties in *State of New York v. Raymond Martinez Fernandez and Martha Jule Beck*, New York Court of Appeals.
2. Brown, Wenzell. *The Lonely Hearts Murders* (1952).
3. Buck, Paul. *The Honeymoon Killers* (1970).
4. Christianson, Scott. *Condemned: Inside the Sing Sing Death House* (2000).
5. Knox, Sarah L. *Murder: A Tale of Modern American Life* (1998).
6. Newspaper reports by *The Daily News* and other contemporary newspapers.
7. Official records of Sing Sing Prison.
8. Trial transcript (Vol. I – VII) and referenced exhibits in *State of New York v. Raymond Martinez Fernandez and Martha Jule Beck*, Bronx County Supreme Court.

A Note on Source Materials

Due to the age of the events of this story, many of the original source materials were long ago discarded or destroyed. Ray and Martha's records from Sing Sing were well maintained. However, police files were no longer available despite multiple requests to the investigating agencies in Michigan and New York. Fortunately, the various statements given by the Lonely Hearts Killers while in police custody in Michigan were preserved as part of the trial proceeding and the record on appeal.

Made in the USA
Columbia, SC
21 August 2022

65817589R00143